T5-BYG-670

BEN JONSON'S
TIMBER OR DISCOVERIES

Ben Jonson's

Timber or *Discoveries*

Ralph S. Walker
University of Aberdeen

Syracuse University Press -- 1953

GEORGE PEABODY COLLEGE
NO LONGER THE PROPERTY OF
VANDERBILT UNIVERSITY LIBRARY
NASHVILLE, TENN.
ENGLISH

CONTENTS

NOTE

Portions of the Introduction to the rearranged edition of *Timber, or Discoveries* appeared in an article in *Essays and Studies of the English Association,* 1952; but I have revised the scheme of rearrangement suggested there and this edition follows the plan laid down in the Introduction, which differs in some respects from that suggested in the article.

The essay on *Jonson's Conversations with Drummond* appeared in *English,* Spring 1952, and is reprinted here by permission; that on the Lyric Poems of Ben Jonson is abbreviated from an article published in *The Criterion,* No. LII. to which I have made considerable alterations.

R. S. W.

INTRODUCTION

MOST READERS of Ben Jonson's *Discoveries* must have found it a somewhat bewildering scrap-book, uneven in quality and apparently wanting in plan, though none can have failed to be impressed by its fitful power and fascination. In parts the paragraphs are linked, for a time, by continuity of sense or similarity of subject-matter: in parts, again, there seems no coherence between them. In his introduction to the edition published in 1906,[1] Professor Castelain called attention to the evidence of a hasty, uncomprehending attempt by some hand, perhaps the first editor's but obviously not the writer's, to group and arrange the assortment of translations, notes, and extracts of which the book is composed. There is plenty of indication that these papers, collected after his death from among Jonson's 'remains,' and assembled under the alternative titles of *Timber, Explorata,* or *Discoveries,* fell at some time into disorder, and it would be easy to give more instances of the glaring misplacement of passages than those mentioned by Castelain or by the most recent co-editors. Professor Herford and Mr. and Mrs. Simpson, being concerned with facts rather than theories, are not prepared to accept Castelain's conclusions about the part played by the editor of the 1640-41 folio in adding to the confusion of the printer's copy, yet an examination of the order and contents of the whole collection has led me to certain opinions about its nature and significance which accord well with most of Castelain's conjectures.

1 *Discoveries: a Critical Edition,* by Maurice Castelain, 1906.

What I think may have happened is that when the so-called Second Folio of 1640-41 was in process of editing, certain sheaves of papers, intended by Jonson for a variety of purposes, but perhaps in few cases for publication exactly as they stood, were collected together and found to be in disorder, or were allowed to fall into disorder in the course of searching through them. The editor, Sir Kenelm Digby, then extracted from among them the fragmentary *Sad Shepherd* and the disorderly *Discoveries,* and decided to add them to Volume II, after the rest of the contents had already gone to press; for, as Castelain points out, these items appear to have been printed separately from the others, and are the only ones in the volume which bear the date 1641. He, or the printer, next, perhaps, made some attempt to reduce the jumbled *Discoveries* to a rough order, and since Jonson had the habit of putting marginal notes and references in Latin to some of his paragraphs, added others where these were lacking, in order to give an air of uniformity to the whole collection. In doing this, as in arranging the order, he did not always pause even to read the passage concerned, and so provided us with the inappropriate headings, of which an example is *Morbi,* for a note[2] whose first line makes figurative mention of diseases, but which is really concerned with the retention of minor errors in ecclesiastical dogma; as also, perhaps, those which merely Latinize the first word or phrase of the passage. The whole thing was then printed, and added to the already prepared third, or critical, section of the volume, to follow *Horace his Art of Poetrie* and the *English Grammar;* just as the *Sad Shepherd* appears to have been added to the fourth, or dramatic section, after the *Magnetic Lady* and the *Tale of a Tub.*

Whether this was precisely what happened or not, it is difficult to escape the conclusion that *Discoveries* was too-hurriedly thrown together and rushed to press. Indeed the whole 'Second Folio' is an example of imperfect editing, and Gifford

[2] Lines 1058-1062: references are to the line-numbers in *Ben Jonson's Works,* edited by Herford and Simpson: Vol. VIII, 1947.

comments, in his note on the *Underwoods,*[3] on its editor's 'rude attempts' to arrange his matter, and the 'marks of carelessness and ignorance' visible in every page. The confusion of the *Discoveries* has been aggravated by subsequent editors, with their different opinions as to paragraphing, and the somewhat misleading system of numbering introduced by Sir Israel Gollancz.[4] But the materials composing it appear to me to be classifiable in seven groups, and I have found it helpful, in studying the book, to keep these groups in mind. First there is a group of five passages on moral topics, to which I am inclined to add a sixth on the pictorial arts, which appear to me to be essays, or portions of essays; second, parts of a work on the writing and appreciation of good literature, intended, it would seem, for the instruction of the young; third, a miscellaneous assortment of scraps of moral wisdom; fourth, a short treatise, or the fragments of a longer one, on statecraft or good government; fifth, a series of notes on poetical theory, with illustrative quotations, written partly in the form of question and answer, which may be lecture-notes intended for expansion and comment by the speaker; sixth, a brief account of the essentials of good letter-writing, drawn up as if at the request of a friend; and last, a few notes of a kind which might be made by a writer of comedies with future plays in mind.

The five, or perhaps six passages in the first group, are longer than those in the third, and show development of thought and signs of shaping from an opening to a conclusion: they appear to be essays composed partly after the manner of Bacon and partly after that of Montaigne. One of these, on the subject of Envy,[5] opens in the Baconian way: "*Envy* is no new thing, nor was it borne onely in our times. The Ages past have brought it forth, and the coming Ages will. So long as there are men fit for it, *quorum odium virtute relicta placet,*[6] it will never be wanting"; but it develops in the more intimate manner of Montaigne, and the style rapidly acquires

3 *The Works of Ben Jonson,* edited by W. Gifford, 1816, Vol. VIII, p. 292.
4 *Timber, or Discoveries,* edited by Israel Gollancz, 1898.
5 Lines 258-321.
6 "whom hatred pleases since they have abandoned virtue."

that warmth of personal feeling which so often distinguishes Jonson's prose from Bacon's. There is no mistaking for Bacon's such a passage as the indignant one which recalls Jonson's taunting Epigram X, *To my Lord Ignorant:*[7] "Hee is upbraydingly call'd a *Poet,* as if it were a most contemptible *Nickname.* But the *Professors* (indeed) have made the learning cheape. Rayling, and tinckling Rimers, whose Writings the vulgar more greedily reade; as being taken with the scurrility, and petulancie of such wits. Hee shall not have a Reader now, unlesse hee jeere and lye. It is the food of men's natures: the diet of the times!" or the passionate outburst later on: "But it is the disease of the Age: and no wonder if the world, growing old, begin to be infirme: Old Age itselfe is a disease. It is long since the sick world began to doate, and talke idly: Woulde she had but doated still; but her dotage is now broke forth into a madnesse, and become a meere phrency."

The essay on Talking Too Much,[8] though derived from a passage in the *Noctes Atticae* of Aulus Gellius, is like the last, complete in itself, and might almost pass for an essay by Bacon, but for the last three sentences, which have that lively colloquial quality often present in Jonson's comic dialogue but entirely foreign to the prose of Bacon: . . . "one, when hee had got the inheritance of an unlucky old *Grange,* would needs sell it; and to draw buyers, proclaim'd the vertues of it. *Nothing* ever thriv'd on it (saith he). *No owner* of it, ever dyed in his bed; some hung, some drown'd themselves; some were banish't, some starv'd; the trees were all blasted; the Swyne dyed of *Measils,* the Cattell of the *Murren,* the Sheepe of the *Rot;* they that stood were ragg'd, bare, and bald as your hand; nothing was ever rear'd there; not a Duckling, or a Goose. *Hospitium fuerat calamitatis.*[9] Was not this man like to sell it?"

7 "Thou call'st me *Poet,* as a terme of shame . . . . . . "
8 Lines 330-404.
9 "It was 'Calamity Inn'."

The passage headed *"Ingeniorum discrimina"* [10] may have been intended for incorporation in the larger discussion of literary styles of which fragments are scattered through the book; but it may equally well have been intended for shaping into an essay of Baconian form on the Diversity of Wits. There can be no doubt as to the prevailing stylistic influence on such sentences as these: "There is no doctrine will doe good, where nature is wanting. Some wits are swelling, and high; others low and still: Some hot and fiery; others cold and dull: One must have a bridle, the other a spurre"; and "You have others that labour onely to ostentation; and are ever more busy about the colours, and surface of a worke, then in the matter, and foundation; For that is hid, the other seene." This essay, as it stands, is largely compounded of scraps translated from Seneca and Quintilian, and what Jonson says in it of essayists, "even their Master *Mountaigne,* who, in all they write, confesse still what bookes they have read last; and therein their owne folly, so much, that they bring it to the *Stake* raw, and undigested," might seem, in view of his own practice, to indicate an abnormal lack of self-criticism in him, if it were not that the emphasis of the passage is on the indiscriminate nature of the borrowing which leads writers into inconsistencies and self-contradiction, whereas Jonson's own borrowings are made with almost unvarying consistency, to illustrate and confirm certain leading principles which he held clearly in mind. Jonson's borrowings are "digested," in the sense that they have been made part of himself, incorporated in his system of thought and belief, before they are produced in translation. We can seldom be quite sure that they are not unconscious recollections from past reading, rather than translations from an open book: for in his *Conversations with Drummond* there are at least four instances of his facility in applying, for his own original purposes, almost the exact words of Latin critics — in references to Drayton, Du Bartas, Lucan, and Beaumont — all made in the course of random

10 Lines 669-800, 846-861, and 948-958.

fireside talk, and showing to what a remarkable degree, as Mr. Patterson says, "he carried the classics in solution in his brain."[11]

The passage rather vaguely headed *"De bonis et malis"* [12] and divided up by five more, equally clumsy, Latin titles in the margin, lacks the initial pounce on the main topic of a typical essay by Bacon, but it develops into a discussion of Worthless Aims which is full both of Baconian reflection and Jonsonian warmth of feeling, and concludes at a high pitch of moral fervour with the clinching aphorism: "Hee that would have his vertue published, is not the servant of vertue, but glory." If these paragraphs, from the *Apologia* of Apuleius and the *Epistolae* of Seneca, do represent an experiment by Jonson in the art of essay-writing, the free, rambling, personal style adopted shows that the model here was not Bacon, except in details, but Montaigne, the "master." The fact that the Latin sources are very closely followed at many points does not lessen the likelihood that the passage was intended for an essay; for, as we have seen, Jonson considered copious borrowing to be a usual process in the compiling of essays, and condemned only those who did not genuinely share the sentiments expressed in their sources.

A passage on the connection between poetry and the pictorial arts which occurs later on in the book [13] and is translated largely from Plutarch and Quintilian, begins as if intended to develop into an essay. If so, it may have been left uncompleted, for instead of rounding-off to an orthodox essay-conclusion, it deteriorates into a summary catalogue of facts: yet even this bare listing of facts has its sanction for a disciple in the practice of Bacon. It is just as possible that it was intended for inclusion among the notes on poetry which seem to form the skeleton of a series of lectures or discourses on the Art of Poetry, and to which several other unattached fragments may belong. As it stands in the folio, it is interrupted

11 *Jonson's Conversations with Drummond,* edited by R. F. Patterson, 1924, Introduction, p. xxxv.
12 Lines 1323-1467.
13 Lines 1509-1540 and 1549-1585.

midway by an irrelevant paragraph[14] which appears to have been inserted on the hasty decision of a casual editor who mistook its first words: "In Picture, light is requir'd no lesse then shadow . . ." to indicate that its contents, like those of the paragraphs before and after, were concerned with the art of painting. The passage which immediately follows that on painting seems to me, on the other hand, to form a complete and shapely little essay on Flatterers,[15] peculiarly interesting because it is so free of the Baconian influence, so comparatively fresh and frank in style, so warm and urgent in its feeling — qualities which may be demonstrated in its final sentences: "Neither will an honourable person inquire, who eats, and drinks together, what that man playes, whom this man loves; with whom such a one walkes; what discourse they held; who sleepes with whom. They are base, and servile natures, that busie themselves about these disquisitions. How often have I seene, (and worthily) these Censors of the family, undertaken by some honest *Rustick,* and cudgel'd thriftily? These are commonly the off-scowring and dregs of men, that doe these things, or calumniate others: Yet I know not truly which is worse; hee that malignes all, or that praises all. There is as great a vice in praising, and as frequent, as in detracting."

The second group of passages is divisible into six sections. I group these together because they are related in subject-matter and similar in style, and I think they may have been intended for incorporation, perhaps with alterations and additions, in a single work. There is the opening of a letter to a patron who has asked for advice and help in the education of his sons;[16] and a series of essays or discourses on diligence in learning, language in oratory, judging the worth of poets and poetry, the value of liberal studies, and how to acquire a good style in writing — all written in a fully-wrought, imaginative, allusive style, and all concerned with teaching about literature

14 Lines 1541-1548.
15 Lines 1586-1635.
16 Lines 1636-1696 and 1787-1820.

and the arts, either theoretically or by more practical instruction. I suggest that here we have an unfinished work intended, like so many other educational writings of the period after the Renaissance, as a textbook for teachers of the young. The introduction would, no doubt, have taken the form of a letter to "My Lord" on the general principles to be observed in the education of children; and on this Jonson has nothing to say that is not thoroughly sound. Ascham, it is true, had said it all before; but Jonson takes from Ascham nothing that is not permanently true and that would not be endorsed by the most enlightened of modern educational theorists. Thereafter the treatise would have been concerned mainly with how and what to read in order to form literary taste; some instructions on how to write well and avoid the stylistic vices common in contemporary authors; and a statement of the principles on which critical judgments of the arts ought to be based.

These extracts, widely dispersed through the *Discoveries* as printed in the folio, can be assembled in several possible sequences so as to reveal a train of thought running through the whole series; and when so assembled they become far more meaningful than when read as fragments in isolation amidst a mass of unrelated matter, and are seen to amount to a consistent presentation of a firmly held critical position. Whether the intention was to combine them into a treatise, or whether they did at one time form a treatise which fell to pieces before it reached the printer, are not matters of so much moment as the fact that they express plainly and without wavering the central corpus of critical belief from which Ben Jonson's thoughts and works alike proceeded.

To the third group I assign forty-one of Sir Israel Gollancz's numbered paragraphs, including the one on the Puritan Hypocrite,[17] which Jonson discreetly phrased in Latin instead of English. These are all short, sententious passages, mostly translated from Latin authors, suitable for rendering into epigrammatic verse or dramatic blank verse according to the plan we know Jonson often followed: many examples can be found in

[17] Lines 60-64.

his plays and poems of versification from Latin originals, and he told Drummond plainly that he wrote his verses first in prose. But they may have been assembled for some other purpose than to provide raw materials for creative writing. They may have been experimental exercises in translation, for their styles vary, and they vary in their closeness to their sources. Some are free, imaginative renderings of their originals, like the translation of Quintilian's "Quantulum enim studiis impartimur? Alias horas vanus salutandi labor, alias datum fabulis otium, alias spectacula, alias convivia trahunt"[18] as "What a deale of cold business doth a man mis-spend the better part of life in! in scattering *complements,* tendring *visits,* gathering and venting *newes,* following *Feasts* and *Playes,* making a little winter-love in a darke corner."[19] Others though suggested by a Latin text, are warm with personal feeling; like the passage on Flattery,[20] which was written with the preface to Book VI of Seneca's *Naturales Quaestiones* in mind. Others, again, though fairly close to their sources, are handled so vividly that they seem direct expressions of personal experience; like the passage on Memory,[21] which it is hard to realize comes almost entirely from Book I of the *Controversiae* of the elder Seneca.

Again, they may have been intended, as has been suggested, merely to fix in the memory, or preserve for reference, notable formulations of the moral sentiments Jonson found peculiarly appealing; but in view of the care, skill, and imaginative energy expended on them, this seems to me unlikely. Certainly they were chosen for their sense, and not for any particular verbal problems to be solved in translation, but though they are brief they are works of conscious art; indeed, the prose in which they are composed is unsurpassed in force and variety by any Jacobean writer. I think it very likely that in this group we have the nucleus of a collection of *apophthegmata,* which Jonson, following the example of Erasmus, was grad-

18 *De Institutione Oratoria,* XII, xi, 18.
19 Lines 56-59.
20 Lines 1070-1092.
21 Lines 479-507.

ually assembling for publication, and to which he intended to apply the characteristically Jonsonian title of *Explorata or Discoveries* subsequently used by the editor of the folio for the whole collection of papers printed as one work at the end of the third section of Volume II. Apart from the influence of the Latin originals, making for dignity and concision, the main influence on their style appears to me to be that of Bacon; and in the composition of these short moral *sententiae* it is naturally the influence of his essay-style, rather than of his more flowing treatise-style which predominates; but in these as in the passages mentioned earlier, Jonson with his long experience as a writer of dramatic dialogue, shows himself more versatile in the management of prose than his model.

The paragraphs in my fourth group appear to belong to a work, roughed out rather than finished off, on the subject of Statecraft. There were plenty of forerunners in this favourite Elizabethan field, and it is difficult to decide from the nature of the fragments in the *Discoveries,* whether Jonson contemplated writing a protracted thesis on the subject, or whether he planned it merely as an anti-Machiavellian tract, or "epistle," expressed on the face of it in terms of state policy, but to be understood more broadly as concerning every man in the conduct of his own affairs. It can hardly be doubted that the fragments belong together, and were collected with one end in view, the style is so consistent, the presence of a theme so obvious, yet they are scattered through the book, and even where they come together in series they are sometimes out of their logical order, as if a hasty attempt had been made to group them, but none to rearrange them in their original sequence. Yet I think they can be assembled in an order which suggests consecutive development of thought and indicates that they were not random and haphazard jottings, but were collected with a plan in mind. It may be that the whole matter of the treatise is here, and that only a linking phrase or two between some of the passages was needed to complete it, before the pages fell into disorder and left the first editor a task of rearrangement, which for some reason, he was unable or unwilling to carry out with any thoroughness. There is here further evidence of Jonson's versatility, and of his habit of experimenting in new literary forms; he was venturing, I suggest, into the field of Sir Thomas Elyot's translations, and had in mind such works as *The Doctrine of Princes* and *The Image of Governance:* but his own treatise, based in part on careful selections from the writings of Vives, Seneca, and Justus Lipsius, would have stressed those qualities in human nature in which he himself most firmly believed, and would have displayed, as anyone must agree who reads the relevant passages in the *Discoveries* consecutively instead of in dispersion as they stand, his own characteristic fervour and pungency.

The fifth group stands intact in the folio[22] (unless some of the earlier critical passages which I have assigned to the second group belong to it) and forms a short *De Poetica,* culled mainly from Aristotle, Cicero, Seneca, Quintilian, Horace, and Daniel Heinsius. It is a framework, rather than a finished treatise or catechism, and it may have been intended as the basis for a fuller written work or for a series of lectures of a formal sort on the accepted theories of art. Illustrative quotations are collected under the various heads, which are framed as questions, and at one point there are some jotted suggestions, undeveloped, as if left for the speaker to elaborate. In some details it repeats the matter of the second group, but it differs in that it is less intimate in style, less personal in the expression of opinion, and it may have been intended primarily as a restatement of the accepted theories of the time from which the speaker might diverge at will. If Jonson lectured for a time in Gresham College, here, perhaps, are some of his lecture-notes.[23]

The sixth group also stands intact in the folio.[24] It is a short essay intended to give clear and practical instruction on how to write a letter in good English. It might conceivably be placed with the essays in the first group; much less suitably

22 Lines 2346-2815.
23 See an article by C. J. Sisson in the *Times Literary Supplement,* Sept. 1951.
24 Lines 2161-2289.

with other instructive matter in the second; but it seems so probable from its manner that it was written separately in answer to a friend's request for advice, that I group it apart.

The seventh and last group is a small one, consisting of thirteen short jottings of a different kind, surely never intended to appear in company with the other materials of the book, or indeed, as they stand, to be published at all. They may have been noted down because of some suggestions they contained which might be of use to a working dramatist always on the look-out for eccentricities of human conduct to portray in comedy, or for a telling, or laughable phrase to leaven his comic dialogue with. Some make little sense: "Of this Spilt water, there is little to bee gathered up: it is a desperate debt":[25] "You admire no *Poems,* but such as run like a Brewers cart upon the stones, hobling".[26] Such scraps are not "publishable matter," yet they may have commended themselves to Jonson because their phrasing suggested figures of speech he might at some time make use of himself. The reprobate husband who preferred drinking and dubious acquaintances to the company of his wife and family;[27] the thief "with a great belly," who longed at the gallow's foot to commit one more robbery;[28] the German Count, who went to trial, torture, and execution always insisting on the ceremony due to his rank;[29] and the "tedious person," with his brainless, irrelevant conversation;[30] might all, conceivably, take shape as characters in a comedy, but they are quite out of place in a prose anthology, in the disjointed, scarcely grammatical form in which they are presented. The sentences of exceedingly trite wisdom, cast in proverbial form, like "Affliction teacheth a wicked person sometimes to pray: *Prosperity* never," [31] and "A woman, the more curious she is about her face, is com-

[25] Lines 195-196.
[26] Lines 2816-2817.
[27] Lines 179-181.
[28] Lines 196-198.
[29] Lines 199-205.
[30] Lines 210-218.
[31] Lines 182-183.

monly the more careless about her house," [32] seem to me equally valueless, except as material for dramatic dialogue, where they might be effectively introduced in suitable situations: and a sentence purporting to explain why the natural instinct of love is stronger than that of hunger, which occurs, in the folio, in the middle of a serious paragraph on the reverence due to princes, is of the same sort. The nonsensical story, headed *"Heare-say Newes,"* about the elephant-ambassador of the Grand Mogul [33] (which I take to be a popular tale invented to explain the significance of the Elephant-and-Castle emblem of the Cutlers' Company, a familiar sight to seventeenth-century Londoners), if it was not copied down from some mere whim, must also surely, have been intended for incorporation in comic dialogue.

With all its variety of content, *Timber or Discoveries* is a work of major significance in English letters. In it Ben Jonson shows himself to be at once the most traditional and the most original critic of his age. He cannot be described as a "neo-classic" critic, unless the term is defined afresh to include his special case, for it is essential to observe that while he has absorbed into the very tissue of his mind much of the best classical teaching about art, he is just as deeply imbued with the spirit of Bacon's *Novum Organum.* Like Bacon's his is a call to the study and imitation of Nature; to experiment and initiative; to emancipation from servile submission to authority; to the use of reason founded on experience for the solution of all problems; to the weighing of facts against theories; to the recognition that learning and art can contribute to the betterment of men's conditions of life. He agrees with Sidney about the high calling of the poet; with Ascham about the value of imitating the best authors; with Harvey about the undesirability of eccentricities in style; with Puttenham about the importance of correction and revision; with Webbe about the causes of the prevalent abuses of language: indeed, it is doubtful if he makes a single point which had not already

32 Lines 192-193.
33 Lines 322-329.

been made by some of his English predecessors. But he differs in that clear-sighted penetration to essentials which saves him from becoming entangled, as they were so prone to be, in superficial matters of decorum, prosody, and diction, and in the integrity which preserves him from academic toying with ideas in the course of a discussion about matters which he felt to be of vital importance. He sees himself as a pioneer, not as a schoolman; and his face is turned, not in humble adoration towards the past, but in energetic optimism towards the future, in spite of those contemporary defections of which he is so sharply aware and which he makes it his business to castigate at every opportunity: "I cannot thinke *Nature* is so spent, and decay'd, that she can bring forth nothing worth her former yeares. She is alwayes the same, like her selfe: And when she collects her strength, is abler still. Men are decay'd, and *studies: Shee is not.*" [34] He is an explorer and discoverer, whose belief is in the virtues of personal experience and practical experiment; and the literary works of the past appeal to him, not as matter for uncritical acceptance and imitation, but as part of that "Nature" which must submit to the scrutiny of the scientific thinker if advances are to be made in knowledge and techniques.

He is classical in the best sense, in that his standards are those of the central current of the humane tradition, continuous though frequently submerged; and have their sanction not merely in the theories of certain classical writers and the practices of others, but in permanent values which are simultaneously moral and aesthetic. His emphasis on such things as "body" in writing, perspicuity, conscious effort and diligent practice, the mean as nearer the truth than the extremes, the desirability of beauty in the surface texture as well as, more profoundly, in the inner meaning of art, is the product of this "central" critical sanity. He has distilled out of the complex mixture of doctrines preached between Plato's time and his own, a simple code, whose key-word is "integrity."

[34] Lines 124-128.

He has, of course, certain limitations, which are inherent in the philosophical vocabulary of his day. We are aware in his thought of that dichotomy of form and subject-matter which was scarcely to be resolved before Coleridge's time: and of the familiar clumsy suggestion that the value of poetry may be judged by its overt moral meaning – a confusion of thought into which Plato betrayed many centuries of critics. But such defects in the instruments available to him are largely surmounted; for in the broad context of his work the blemishes and inconsistencies due to contemporary limitations of thought are absorbed and to a great extent adjusted.

In the *Discoveries* we have the key to his own aims as pursued along many different paths, as well as to that unrecorded body of teaching which so profoundly impressed his disciples and was imparted largely orally in one tavern supper-room or another. He was a conscious artist, not merely in the "bricklayer" sense, but in the sense that his art was consciously directed towards the fulfilment of certain firmly held beliefs and ideals He was not equally successful in all the lines of experiment he adopted; but in all alike he was driven by the need, not only to express his critical ideas, but to embody in words the underlying classical conception of truth and beauty of which both his critical theories and his moral beliefs were products. In this he seems to me unique among the poets of his day, for in him alone I find clear evidence that the intellectual, ratiocinative processes of the mind were as keenly alert as the creative impulses and in general harmony with them.

He was conscious, as a follower of Bacon could not fail to be, of his situation in a changing world; and his awareness of the tendencies of his time, as products of men's thoughts and actions and so within the power of men to guide, gave him a strong sense of responsibility towards society, and a desire to evoke the same conscientiousness in his contemporaries. He could not help being a propagandist, in his art, in his criticism, and in his conversation. And because he was so strongly aware of the relationship which exists between moral and social tendencies and the trends of literary taste and practice, he could not help being as much a moralist and social reformer as he was a literary critic. Writing was his special activity, and he conceives himself as performing for literature a work analogous to Bacon's work for learning in general; but the field of literature is broad, and in his drama, in his epigrammatic and occasional verse, and in his prose essays, he finds opportunities to exercise the moral and social critic in him alongside the literary critic and stylist. In the best of his lyric poetry, as I have tried to show elsewhere, he does something more. There theory and practice are at one, absorbed in creative activity, so that the springs of both are revealed, and the underlying classical conception of the nature of truth and beauty, which, in one way or another, actuates nearly all his work, is realized in complete and satisfying form.

Swinburne called attention to the *Discoveries* in terms of the highest enthusiasm, as a little-known work deserving the utmost praise, and rated it above the *Essays* of Bacon as "superior in truth of insight, breadth of view, vigour of reflection and concision of eloquence." [35] He was apparently not aware that the book consisted largely of translations, some free, some close, from Latin authors, and the warmth of his praise for it as an original work had a curiously harmful effect on its reputation; for when later critics assembled and displayed the source-passages of Jonson's widespread borrowings, it was almost as if false pretensions had been unveiled and a piece of most presumptuous plagiarizing laid bare. Of course no such thing had really happened; but because the book may have come to be undervalued by some as a result, I have tried to show what I think its originality and significance do consist in.

It should not, I am convinced, be regarded as a mere haphazard collection of *Loci Critici*, compiled from unrelated scraps thrown together at random. It contains an assortment of short aphoristic passages, many of them striking examples of vivid translation into pithy, imaginative prose, which may

35 *A Study of Ben Jonson*, by Algernon Charles Swinburne, 1889.

be the nucleus of a projected work after the manner of several such compilations by Erasmus. It also contains, I maintain, the makings of an anti-Machiavellian treatise on statecraft; and a number of completed essays on moral topics, written in a style so rich and varied, and moving with such assurance over so great a range between the grandiloquent and the comic-colloquial, between the passionate and the impersonal, that the writer might fairly claim first place among Jacobean prose-stylists. And most important of all, it contains a body of consistent critical thought, the study of which is essential to the understanding of Jonson's mind and art, and which constitutes it a work of major significance in the history of English criticism. Moreover it has, even now, in spite of the archaic idom of its thought, a message of sanity and grace that writers and readers of today might do well to lay to heart.

In preparing this edition of the *Discoveries,* rearranged in seven sections according to my analysis of the nature of its contents, I have followed the original text of the "Second Folio" of 1640-41, without verbal alterations or emendations, except in the few places where these are quite obviously called for because of some slip or omission in the printing.

Since this is not an antiquarian's edition, and no reader making a textual study of the work will rely on it alone, I have aimed at clarifying style and meaning by modernizing the spelling and punctuation. Few readers intent on the sense and style of such a work would labour to read it in the pronunciation of the seventeenth century: conventions of spelling and punctuation have changed as habits of pronunciation have, and in such an edition as this there is a good case, I think, for removing the superficial barriers to comprehension and appreciation set up for the modern reader by these antiquated conventions.

I have also omitted a great many of the marginal Latin tags and titles, for these are often of no assistance in the reading of the text, and appear to be there in some cases merely for ease of reference, in others as a result of the first editor's desire to give a uniform appearance to a jumbled and incoherent mass of manuscript. I have given English titles to the sections and subsections, and these are not intended to be decorative but merely to indicate the nature of the contents.

In making the rearrangement I have had, occasionally, to be bold in choosing one of several alternative possibilities, knowing that valid objections might be made; as for instance where I have inserted short paragraphs from one part of the book in the middle of longer passages in another part, and where I have divided portions reasonably consecutive as they stand. But the first editor's methods in scrambling his materials have necessitated rather similar methods in the attempt to unscramble them.

Though this edition was planned before the notes to Herford and Simpson's text of the *Discoveries* appeared, my debt to them is enormous, and I have profited both from their researches into the source-matter of Jonson's borrowings and from their handling of the text.

TIMBER, or DISCOVERIES

Made upon Men and Matter,
as they have flowed out of his daily Readings,
or had their reflux to his peculiar Notions of the Times.

By BEN JONSON

Tecum habita, ut noris quam sit tibi curta supellex:

Pers. sat. 4.[1]

The whole text rearranged as follows:

I. Essays:
1. Of Flatterers.
2. Of the Diversity of Wits.
3. Of Envy.
4. Of Talking Overmuch.
5. Of Worthless Aims.
6. Of Picture and Poetry.

II. Of Learning to Read Well, Speak Well and Write Well:
1. Introductory Letter.
2. Of Diligence in Learning.
3. Of Language in Oratory.
4. Of Judging Poets and Poetry.
5. Of Liberal Studies.
6. Of Writing Well.

III. Explorata.

IV. Of Statecraft.

V. The Art of Poetry.

VI. Of Letter Writing.

VII. Random Notes.

1 "Live at home to realize how poorly your house is furnished," Juvenal.

I. ESSAYS

1. Of Flatterers

There are flatterers for their bread, that praise all my oraculous Lord does or says, be it true or false; invent tales that shall please; make baits for his Lordship's ears, and if they be not received in what they offer at, they shift a point of the compass and turn their tale, presently tack about, deny what they confessed and confess what they denied; fit their discourse to the persons and occasions; what they snatch up and devour at one table utter at another, and grow suspected of the master, hated of the servants; while they enquire, and reprehend, and compound, and delate business of the house they have nothing to do with. They praise my Lord's wine and the sauce he likes; observe the cook and bottle-man; while they stand in my Lord's favour, speak for a pension for them, but pound them to dust upon my Lord's least distaste or change of his palate.

How much better is it to be silent, or at least to speak sparingly! For it is not enough to speak good, but timely things. If a man be asked a question, to answer, but to repeat the question before he answer, is well, that he be sure to understand it, to avoid absurdity. For it is less dishonour to hear imperfectly than to speak imperfectly. The ears are excused: the understanding is not. And in things unknown to a man, not to give his opinion, lest by affectation of knowing too much he lose the credit he hath, by speaking or knowing the wrong way what he utters. Nor seek to get his patron's favour by embarking himself in the factions of the family, to enquire after domestic simulties,[1] their sports or affections. They are an odious and vile kind of creatures that fly about the house all day, and picking up the filth of the house, like pies[2] or swallows, carry it to their nest (the lord's ears) and often-times report the lies they have feigned for what they have seen and heard.

1 quarrels
2 magpies

These are called instruments of grace and power, with great persons, but they are indeed the organs of their impotency and marks of weakness. For sufficient lords are able to make these discoveries themselves. Neither will an honourable person enquire who eats and drinks together; what that man plays; whom this man loves; with whom such a one walks; what discourse they held; who sleeps with whom. They are base and servile natures that busy themselves about these disquisitions. How often have I seen, and worthily, these censors of the family undertaken by some honest rustic and cudgelled thriftily! [3] These are commonly the off-scouring and dregs of men that do these things, or calumniate others: yet I know not truly which is worse, he that maligns all or that praises all. There is as great a vice in praising, and as frequent, as in detracting.

2. Of the Diversity of Wits

In the difference of wits, I have observed, there are many notes,[4] and it is a little maistry[5] to know them, to discern what every nature, every disposition, will bear: for before we sow our land we should plough it. There are no fewer forms of minds than of bodies amongst us. The variety is incredible, and therefore we must search. Some are fit to make divines, some poets, some lawyers, some physicians, some to be sent to the plough and trades.

There is no doctrine will do good where nature is wanting. Some wits are swelling and high, others low and still; some hot and fiery, others cold and dull: one must have a bridle, the other a spur.

There be some that are forward and bold, and these will do every little thing easily — I mean that is hard by and next them — which they will utter unretarded, without any shamefacedness. These never perform much, but quickly. They are what they are on the sudden: they show presently like grain that, scattered on the top of the ground, shoots up, but takes

3 thoroughly
4 outward signs
5 mastery (as of an art or skill)

no root; has a yellow blade, but the ear empty. They are wits of good promise at first, but there is an *ingenistitium* (a wit-stand): they stand still at sixteen, they get no higher.

You have others that labour only to ostentation and are ever more busy about the colours and surface of a work than in the matter and foundation: for that is hid, the other seen. Others that in composition are nothing but what is rough and broken: *Quae per salebras, altaque saxa cadunt.*[6] And if it would come gently, they trouble it of purpose. They would not have it run without rubs, as if that style were more strong and manly that struck the ear with a kind of unevenness. These men err not by chance, but knowingly and willingly: they are like men that affect a fashion by themselves, have some singularity in a ruff, cloak, or hat-band, or their beards specially cut to provoke beholders and set a mark upon themselves. They would be reprehended, while they are looked on. And this vice, one that is in authority with the rest loving, delivers over to them to be imitated; so that oft-times the faults which he fell into, the others seek for. This is the danger, when vice becomes a precedent.

Others there are that have no composition at all, but a kind of tuning and rhyming fall in what they write. It runs and slides and only makes a sound. Women's poets they are called, as you have women's tailors.

They write a verse as smooth, as soft, as cream;
In which there is no torrent, nor scarce stream.

You may sound these wits and find the depth of them with your middle finger. They are cream-bowl, or but puddle deep.

Some that turn over all books and are equally searching in all papers, that write out of what they presently find or meet, without choice – by which means it happens that what they have discredited and impugned in one work, they have before, or after, extolled the same in another. Such are all the essayists, even their master, Montaigne. These, in all they write, confess still what books they have read last, and therein their own folly so much that they bring it to the stake raw and

[6] "that pass over rough roads and great rocks": Martial, *Epig.* XI, 90.

undigested: not that the place did need it neither, but that they thought themselves furnished and *would* vent it.

Some again, who, after they have got authority, or, which is less, opinion, by their writings, to have read much, dare presently to feign whole books and authors, and lie safely. For what never was will not easily be found, not by the most curious.

And some, by a cunning protestation against all reading, and false venditation[7] of their own naturals,[8] think to divert the sagacity of their readers from themselves and cool the scent of their own fox-like thefts, when yet they are so rank as a man may find whole pages together usurped from one author, their necessities compelling them to read for present use, which could not be in many books, and so come forth more ridiculously and palpably guilty than those who, because they cannot trace, they yet would slander their industry.

But the wretcheder are the obstinate contemners of all helps and arts, such as presuming on their own naturals (which perhaps are excellent) dare deride all diligence, and seem to mock at the terms when they understand not the things, thinking that way to get off wittily with their ignorance. These are imitated often by such as are their peers in negligence, though they cannot be in nature; and they utter all they can think, with a kind of violence and indisposition, unexamined, without relation either to person, place, or any fitness else. And the more wilful and stubborn they are in it, the more learned they are esteemed of the multitude, through their excellent vice of judgment, who think those things the stronger that have no art, as if to break were better than to open, or to rend asunder, gentler than to loose.

It cannot but come to pass that these men, who commonly seek to do more than enough, may sometimes happen on something that is good and great, but very seldom; and when it comes, it doth not recompense the rest of their ill. For their jests and their sentences (which they only, and ambitiously

7 ostentatious display
8 natural gifts

seek for) stick out and are more eminent because all is sordid and vile about them, as lights are more discerned in a thick darkness than a faint shadow. Now because they speak all they can, however unfitly, they are thought to have the greater copy; where the learned use ever election and a mean – they[9] look back to what they intended at first, and make all an even and proportioned body. The true artificer will not run away from nature, as he were afraid of her, or depart from life and the likeness of truth, but speak to the capacity of his hearers. And though his language differ from the vulgar somewhat, it shall not fly from all humanity, with the Tamburlaines and Tambur-Chams[10] of the late age, which had nothing in them but the scenical strutting and furious vociferation to warrant them to the ignorant gapers. He knows it is his only art so to carry it as none but artificers perceive it. In the meantime, perhaps, he is called barren, dull, lean, a poor writer, or by what contumelious word can come in their cheeks, by these men who, without labour, judgment, knowledge, or almost sense, are received or preferred before him. He gratulates them and their fortune. Another age, or juster men, will acknowledge the virtues of his studies, his wisdom in dividing, his subtlety in arguing; with what strength he doth inspire his readers, with what sweetness he strikes them; in inveighing what sharpness, in jest what urbanity he uses; how he doth reign in men's affections, how invade and break in upon them, and makes their minds like the thing he writes. Then in his elocution to behold what word is proper, which hath ornament, which height, what is beautifully translated, where figures are fit, which gentle, which strong to show the composition manly; and how he hath avoided faint, obscure, obscene, sordid, humble, improper, or effeminate phrase, which is not only praised of the most, but commended, which is worse, especially for that it is naught.

9 i.e. the learned.

10 Referring to Marlowe's *Tamburlaine the Great* and all such highly rhetorical dramas with an oriental setting. Folio has *Tamerlanes, and Tamer-chams,* with perhaps a punning significance in *Tamer.*

It is no wonder men's eminence appears but in their own way. Virgil's felicity left him in prose, as Tully's forsook him in verse. Sallust's orations are read in the honour of story, yet the most eloquent Plato's speech, which he made for Socrates is neither worthy or[11] the patron, or the person defended. Nay, in the same kind of oratory, and where the matter is one, you shall have him that reasons strongly open negligently, another that prepares well not fit so well; and this happens not only to brains but to bodies. One can wrestle well, another run well, a third leap or throw the bar, a fourth lift or stop a cart going; each hath his way of strength. So in other creatures: some dogs are for the deer, some for the wild boar, some are fox-hounds, some otter-hounds. Nor are all horses for the coach or saddle; some are for the cart and panniers.

There cannot be one colour of the mind, another of the wit. If the mind be staid, grave, and composed, the wit is so; that vitiated, the other is blown and deflowered. Do we not see if the mind languish the members are dull? Look upon an effeminate person; his very gait confesseth him. If a man be fiery, his motion is so; if angry, 'tis troubled and violent. So that we may conclude: wheresoever manners and fashions are corrupted, language is. It imitates the public riot. The excess of feasts and apparel are the notes of a sick state, and the wantonness of language, of a sick mind.

3. Of Envy

Envy is no new thing, nor was it born only in our times. The ages past have brought it forth and the coming ages will. So long as there are men fit for it, *quorum odium virtute relicta placet,*[12] it will never be wanting. It is a barbarous envy to take from those men's virtues which, because thou canst not arrive at, thou impotently despaires[t] to imitate. Is it a crime in me that I know that which others had not yet known but from me; or that I am the author of many things which

11 Cornwall conj. *of*

12 "to whom hatred is pleasing, since they have abandoned virtue." V. J. Scaliger.

never would have come in thy thought but that I taught them? It is a new, but a foolish way you have found out, that whom you cannot equal or come near in doing, you would destroy or ruin with evil speaking, as if you had bound both your wits and natures prentices to slander, and then came forth the best artificers when you could form the foulest calumnies.

Indeed, nothing is of more credit or request now than a petulant paper, or scoffing verses, and it is but convenient to the times and manners we live with to have then the worst writings and studies flourish when the best begin to be despised. Ill arts begin where good end.

The time was when men would learn and study good things, not envy those that had them. Then men were had in price for learning; now letters only make men vile. He is upbraidingly called "a poet," as if it were a most contemptible nickname. But the professors, indeed, have made the learning cheap—railing and tinkling rhymers, whose writings the vulgar more greedily read, as being taken with the scurrility and petulancy of such wits. He shall not have a reader now, unless he jeer and lie. It is the food of men's natures, the diet of the times! Gallants cannot sleep else. The writer must lie, and the gentle reader rests happy to hear the worthiest works misinterpreted, the clearest actions obscured, the innocentest life traduced; and in such a license of lying, a field so fruitful of slanders, how can there be matter wanting to his laughter? Hence comes the epidemical infection, for how can they escape the contagion of the writings whom the virulency of the calumnies hath not staved off from reading?

Nothing doth more invite a greedy reader than an unlooked-for subject; and what more unlooked-for than to see a person of an unblamed life made ridiculous, or odious, by the artifice of lying. But it is the disease of the age, and no wonder if the world, growing old, begin to be infirm: old age itself is a disease. It is long since the sick world began to doat and talk idly. Would she had but doted still: but her dotage is now broke forth into a madness and become a mere frenzy.

This *Alastor*,[13] who hath left nothing unsearched, or unassailed by his impudent and licentious lying in his aguish writings (for he was in his cold quaking fit all the while), what hath he done more than a troublesome base cur – barked and made a noise afar off, had a fool or two to spit in his mouth and cherish him with a musty bone? But they are rather enemies of my fame than me, these barkers.

It is an art to have so much judgment as to apparel a lie well, to give it a good dressing, that though the nakedness would show deformed and odious, the suiting of it might draw their readers. Some love any strumpet, be she never so shoplike or meritorious,[14] in good clothes. But these, nature could not have formed them better to destroy their own testimony and overthrow their calumny.

4. Of Talking Overmuch

A wise tongue should not be licentious and wandering, but moved and, as it were, governed with certain reins from the heart and bottom of the breast, and it was excellently said of that philosopher,[15] that there was a wall, or parapet of teeth set in our mouth to restrain the petulancy of our words, that the rashness of talking should not only be retarded by the guard and watch of our heart, but be fenced in and defended by certain strengths placed in the mouth itself and within the lips. But you shall see some so abound with words without any seasoning or taste of matter in so profound a security as while they are speaking, for the most part, they confess to speak they know not what.

Of the two, if either were to be wished, I would rather have a plain, downright wisdom than a foolish and affected eloquence. For what is so furious and bedlam-like as a vain sound of chosen and excellent words without any subject of sentence or science mixed?

13 An anonymous critic.
14 Whalley conj. *meretricious*
15 Plutarch, *De Garrulitate.*

Whom the disease of talking still once possesseth, he can never hold his peace. Nay, rather than he will not discourse, he will hire men to hear him; and so heard, not harkened unto, he comes off most times like a mountebank that when he hath praised his medicines finds none will take them or trust him. He is like Homer's Thersites, *ametroepes, akritomuthos,* speaking without judgment or measure. *Loquax magis, quam facundus. Satis loquentiae, sapientiae parum.*[16]

Glosses toi thesauros en anthropoisin aristos
Pheidoles pleiste de charis kata metron iouses.[17]
Optimus est homini linguae thesaurus, et ingens
Gratia, quae parcis mensurat singula verbis.[18]

Ulysses, in Homer, is made a long-thinking man before he speaks, and Epaminondas is celebrated by Pindar to be a man that, though he knew much, yet he spoke but little. Demaratus, when on the Bench he was long silent and said nothing, one asking him if it were folly in him or want of language, he answered, "A fool could never hold his peace." For too much talking is ever the *indice* of a fool.

Dum tacet indoctus, poterit cordatus haberi;
Is morbos animi namque tacendo tegit.[19]

Nor is that worthy speech of Zeno the philosopher to be past over without the note of ignorance, who being invited to a feast in Athens, where a great prince's ambassadors were entertained, and was the only person had said nothing at the table, one of them with courtesy asked him, "What shall we return from thee, Zeno, to the Prince, our master, if he ask us of thee?" "Nothing," he replied, "more, but that you found an old man in Athens that knew to be silent amongst his cups." It was near a miracle, to see an old man silent, since talking is the disease of age: but amongst cups makes it fully a wonder.

16 "Wordy, rather than eloquent. Plenty speech, but little wisdom." Sallust.
17 "The greatest treasure is a sparing tongue; the greatest grace, a moderate one," Hesiod.
18 A Latin rendering of the preceding passage in Greek.
19 "The dunce seems knowing whilst he conceals his ignorance by silence."

It was wittily said upon one that was taken for a great and grave man so long as he held his peace: "This man might have been a counsellor of state, till he spoke: but having spoken, not the beadle of the ward." *Echemuthia Pythag-[orae] quam laudabilis!*[20] *Glosses pro ton allon kratei, theois hepomenos.*[21] *Linguam cohibe, prae aliis omnibus, ad Deorum exemplum.*[22] *Digito compesce labellum.*[23]

There is almost no man but he sees clearlier and sharper the vices in a speaker, than the virtues. And there are many that with more ease will find fault with what is spoken foolishly than that can give allowance to that wherein you are wise silently. "The treasure of a fool is always in his tongue," said the witty comic poet,[24] and it appears not in anything more than in the notion whereof one, when he had got the inheritance of an unlucky old grange, would needs sell it, and to draw buyers proclaimed the virtues of it. "Nothing ever thrived on it," saith he. "No owner of it ever died in his bed: some hung, some drowned themselves, some were banished, some starved. The trees were all blasted; the swine died of the measles,[25] the cattle of the murrain, the sheep of the rot; they that stood were ragged, bare, and bald as your hand. Nothing was ever reared there, not a duckling or a goose. *Hospitium fuerat calamitatis.*" [26] Was not this man like to sell it?

20 "How admirable is Pythagorean silence!"
21 "In obedience to the gods, master your tongue." Apuleius.
22 A Latin rendering of the preceding passage in Greek.
23 "Press your lip with your finger." Juvenal
24 Plautus in *Poenulus* III, 3. The piece of dialogue which follows is freely adapted from Act II of the *Trinummus.*
25 A disease in swine which is produced by the tapeworm.
26 "It was 'Calamity Inn'."

5. Of Worthless Aims

A good man will avoid the spot of any sin. The very aspersion is grievous, which makes him choose his way in his life as he would in his journey. The ill man rides through all confidently; he is coated and booted for it. The oftener he offends, the more openly and the fouler, the fitter in fashion. His modesty like a riding coat the more it is worn is the less cared for. It is good enough for the dirt still and the ways he travels in. An innocent man needs no eloquence; his innocence is instead of it, else I had never come off so many times from these precipices whither men's malice hath pursued me. It is true, I have been accused to the Lords, to the King, and by great ones; but it happened my accusers had not thought of the accusation with themselves, and so were driven, for want of crimes, to use invention, which was found slander; or too late, being entered so far, to seek starting-holes for their rashness which were not given them. And then they may think what accusation that was like to prove, when they that were the engineers feared to be the authors. Nor were they content to feign things against me, but to urge things feigned by the ignorant against my profession, which though from their hired and mercenary impudence I might have passed by, as granted to a nation of barkers that let out their tongues to lick others' sores, yet I durst not leave myself undefended, having a pair of ears unskilful to hear lies, or have those things said of me which I could truly prove of them. They objected making of verses to me, when I could object to most of them their not being able to read them but as worthy of scorn. Nay, they would offer to urge mine own writings against me, but by pieces, which was an excellent way of malice, as if any man's context might not seem dangerous and offensive if that which was knit to what went before were defrauded of his beginning, or that things by themselves uttered might not seem subject to calumny which read entire would appear most free. At last they upbraided my poverty. I confess she is my domestic, sober of diet, simple of habit, frugal, painful, a good counsellor to me that keeps me from cruelty, pride, or other more delicate impertinences which are the nurse-children of riches. But let them look over all the great and monstrous wickednesses, they shall never find those in poor families. They are the issue of the wealthy giants and the mighty hunters; whereas no great work, or worthy of praise or memory, but came out of poor cradles. It was the ancient poverty that founded commonweals, built cities, invented arts, made wholesome laws, armed men against vices, rewarded them with their own virtues, and preserved the honour and state of nations, till they betrayed themselves to riches.

Money never made any man rich, but his mind. He that can order himself to the law of nature is not only without the sense but the fear of poverty. O! but to strike blind the people with our wealth and pomp is the thing! What a wretchedness is this, to thrust all our riches outward and be beggars within; to contemplate nothing but the little, vile, and sordid things of the world, not the great, noble, and precious! We serve our avarice, and not content with the good of the earth that is offered us, we search and dig for the evil that is hidden. God offered us those things, and placed them at hand and near us, that he knew were profitable for us; but the hurtful he laid deep and hid. Yet do we seek only the things whereby we may perish, and bring them forth, when God and nature hath buried them. We covet superfluous things, when it were more honour for us if we could contemn necessary. What need hath nature of silver dishes, multitude of waiters, delicate pages, perfumed napkins? She requires meat only, and hunger is not ambitious. Can we think no wealth enough but such a state for which a man may be brought into a *praemunire*,[27] begged, proscribed, or poisoned? O! if a man could restrain the fury of his gullet and groin, and think how many fires, how many kitchens, cooks, pastures and ploughed lands, what orchards, stews,[28] ponds and parks, coops and garners he could spare; what velvets, tissues, embroideries, laces he could lack; and then how short and uncertain his life is, he were in a bet-

27 summonsed
28 tanks for storing fish

ter way to happiness than to live the emperor of these delights and be the dictator of fashions! But we make ourselves slaves to our pleasures, and we serve fame and ambition, which is an equal slavery. Have I not seen the pomp of a whole kingdom, and what a foreign king could bring hither also to make himself gazed and wondered at, laid forth as it were to the show, and vanish all away in a day? [29] And shall that which could not fill the expectation of few hours entertain and take up our whole lives, when even it appeared as superfluous to the possessors as to me that was a spectator? The bravery was shown, it was not possessed; while it boasted itself it perished. It is vile and a poor thing to place our happiness on these desires. Say we wanted them all: famine ends famine.[30]

There is nothing valiant or solid to be hoped for from such as are always kempt and perfumed and every day smell of the tailor, the exceedingly curious, that are wholly in[31] mending such an imperfection in the face, in taking away the morphew[32] in the neck, or bleaching their hands at midnight, gumming and bridling their beards, or making the waist small, binding it with hoops, while the mind runs at waste. Too much pickedness[33] is not manly. Nor from those that will jest at their own outward imperfections, but hide their ulcers within, their pride, lust, envy, ill-nature, with all the art and authority they can. These persons are in danger, for whilst they think to justify their ignorance by impudence, and their persons by clothes and outward ornaments, they use but a commission to deceive themselves: where [as], if we will look with our understanding, and not our senses, we may behold virtue and beauty, though covered with rags, in their brightness, and vice and deformity so much the fouler in having all the splendour of riches to gild them, or the false light of honour and power to help them. Yet this is that wherewith

29 The feasts and pageants at the wedding of the Princess Elizabeth, daughter of James VI to Frederick, Elector Palatine, in February 1613, cost the Exchequer £60,000.

30 "famine ends in starvation."

31 set on

32 a skin eruption

33 fastidiousness

the world is taken, and runs mad to gaze on: clothes and titles, the birdlime of fools.

What petty things they are we wonder at: like children, that esteem every trifle and prefer a fairing before their fathers! What difference is between us and them, but that we are dearer fools, coxcombs at a higher rate? They are pleased with cockleshells, whistles, hobby-horses, and such like: we with statues, marble pillars, pictures, gilded roofs, where underneath is lathe and lime, perhaps loam. Yet we take pleasure in the lie, and are glad we can cosen[34] ourselves. Nor is it only in our walls and ceilings, but all that we call happiness is mere painting and gilt, and all for money. What a thin membrane of honour that is! And how hath all true reputation fallen since money began to have any! Yet the great herd, the multitude, that in all other things are divided, in this alone conspire and agree: to love money. They wish for it and embrace it; they adore it, while yet it is possessed with greater stir and torment than it is gotten.

Some men, what losses soever they have, they make them greater; and if they have none, even all that is not gotten is a loss. Can there be creatures of more wretched condition than these, that continually labour under their own misery and others' envy? A man should study other things, not to covet, not to fear, not to repent him: to make his base such as no tempest shall shake him, to be secure of all opinion and pleasing to himself, even for that wherein he displeaseth others. For the worst opinion gotten for doing well should delight us: wouldst not thou be just, but for fame, thou oughtst [35] to be it with infamy. He that would have his virtue published is not the servant of virtue, but glory.[36]

34 deceive
35 i.e. deservedst.
36 i.e. vainglory.

6. Of Picture and Poetry

Poetry and picture[37] are arts of a like nature and both are busy about imitation. It was excellently said of Plutarch, poetry was a speaking picture and picture a mute poesie; for they both invent, feign, and devise many things, and accommodate all they invent to the use and service of nature. Yet of the two, the pen is more noble than the pencil; for that can speak to the understanding, the other but to the sense. They both behold pleasure and profit as their common object, but should abstain from all base pleasures, lest they should err from their end, and while they seek to better men's minds destroy their manners. They both are born artificers, not made. Nature is more powerful in them than study.

Whosoever loves not picture is injurious to truth and all the wisdom of poetry. Picture is the invention of heaven, the most ancient and most akin to nature. It is itself a silent work, and always of one and the same habit, yet it doth so enter and penetrate the inmost affection (being done by an excellent artificer) as sometimes it overcomes the power of speech and oratory. There are diverse graces in it: so are there in the artificers. One excels in care, another in reason, a third in easiness, a fourth in nature and grace. Some have diligence and comeliness, but they want majesty: they can express a human form in all the graces, sweetness, and elegancy, but they miss the authority: they can hit nothing but smooth cheeks, they cannot express roughness or gravity. Others aspire to truth so much as they are rather lovers of likeness than beauty.

Zeuxis and Parrhasius[38] are said to be contemporaries: the first found out the reason of lights and shadows in picture, the other more subtly examined the lines. Picture took her feigning from poetry: from geometry her rule, compass, lines, proportion, and the whole symmetry. Parrhasius was the first won reputation by adding symmetry to picture: he added subtlety to the countenance, elegancy to the hair, loveliness to

[37] the pictorial arts
[38] Greek painters of the 5th century B.C., both famed for their realism.

the face, and, by the public voice of all artificers, deserved honour in the outer lines. Eupompus[39] gave it splendour by numbers and other elegancies. From the optics it drew reasons, by which it considered how things placed at distance and afar off should appear less, how above or beneath the head should deceive the eye, etc. So from thence it took shadows, recessor,[40] light and heightenings. From moral philosophy it took the soul, the expression of senses, perturbations, manners, when they would paint an angry person, a proud, an inconstant, an ambitious, a brave, a magnanimous, a just, a merciful, a compassionate, an humble, a dejected, a base, and the like. They made all heightenings bright, all shadows dark, all swellings from a plane, all solids from breaking. See where he (Vitruvius, viii, 7) complains of their painting chimaeras, by the vulgar inaptly called "grotesque," saying that men who were born truly to study and emulate nature did nothing but make monsters against nature, which Horace so laughed at. The art plastic was moulding in clay or potter's earth anciently. This is the parent of statuary: sculpture, graving and picture, cutting in brass and marble, all serve under her. Socrates taught Parrhasius and Clito, two noble statuaries, first to express manners by their looks in imagery. Polygnotus and Aglaophon[41] were ancienter: after them, Zeuxis, who was the lawgiver to all painters after Parrhasius. They were contemporaries and lived both about Philip's time, the father of Alexander the Great.

There lived in this latter age six famous painters in Italy who were excellent and emulous of the ancients: Raphael de Urbino, Michel Angelo Buonarotta, Titian, Antonio of Correggio, Sebastian of Venice, Julio Romano, and Andrea del Sarto.

39 Greek painter of the 5th century B.C., who founded the Sicyonian school.

40 Schelling conj. *recession,* i.e. perspective.

41 Greek painters of the 5th century B.C., praised by Quintilian.

II. OF LEARNING TO READ WELL, SPEAK WELL, AND WRITE WELL

1. Introductory Letter

It pleased your Lordship of late to ask my opinion touching the education of your sons, and especially to the advancement of their studies: to which, though I returned somewhat for the present which rather manifested a will in me than gave any just resolution to the thing propounded, I have upon better cogitation called those aids about me, both of mind and memory, which shall venture[1] my thoughts clearer, if not fuller, to your Lordship's demand. I confess, my Lord, they will seem but petty and minute things I shall offer to you, being writ for children, and of them. But studies have their infancy as well as creatures. We see in men, even the strongest compositions had their beginnings from milk and the cradle, and the wisest tarried sometimes about apting their mouths to letters and syllables.

In their education, therefore, the care must be the greater had of their beginnings, to know, examine, and weigh their natures, which though they be proner in some children to some disciplines, yet are they naturally prompt to taste all by degrees and with change. For change is a kind of refreshing in studies, and infuseth knowledge by way of recreation. Thence the school itself is called a play or game, and all letters are so best taught to scholars. They should not be affrighted or deterred in their entry, but drawn on with exercise and emulation. A youth should not be made to hate study before he know the causes to love it, or taste the bitterness before the sweet, but called on and allured, entreated and praised; yea, when he deserves it not.

For which cause I wish them sent to the best school, and a public, which I think the best. Your Lordship, I fear, hardly hears of that, as willing to breed them in your eye and at home, and doubting their manners may be corrupted abroad. They are in more danger in your own family, among ill ser-

1 Folio has *venter*.

vants (allowing they be safe in their schoolmaster) than amongst a thousand boys, however immodest. Would we did not spoil our own children and overthrow their manners ourselves by too much indulgence! To breed them at home is to breed them in a shade, where in a school they have the light and heat of the sun. They are used and accustomed to things and men. When they come forth into the commonwealth, they find nothing new or to seek. They have made their friendships and aids, some to last till their age. They hear what is commanded to others as well as themselves much approved, much corrected, all which they bring to their own store and use, and learn as much as they hear. Eloquence would be but a poor thing if we should only converse with singulars,[2] speak but man and man together. Therefore I like no private breeding. I would send them where their industry should be daily increased by praise, and that kindled by emulation. It is a good thing to inflame the mind, and though ambition itself be a vice, it is often the cause of great virtue. Give me that wit whom praise excites, glory puts on, or disgrace grieves: he is to be nourished with ambition, pricked forward with honour, checked with reprehension, and never to be suspected of sloth. Though he be given to play, it is a sign of spirit and liveliness; so there be a mean had of their sports and relaxations. And from the rod or ferule I would have them free, as from the menace of them: for it is both deformed and servile.

Therefore youth ought to be instructed betimes and in the best things: for we hold those longest we take soonest, as the first scent of a vessel lasts, and that tinct the wool first receives. Therefore a master should temper his own powers and descend to the other's infirmity. If you pour a glut of water upon a bottle it receives little of it, but with a funnel, and by degrees, you shall fill many of them and spill little of your own: to their capacity they will all receive and be full.

And as it is fit to read the best authors to youth first, so let them be of the openest and clearest, as Livy before Sallust, Sidney before Donne; and beware of letting them taste Gower

2 single individuals

or Chaucer at first, lest falling too much in love with antiquity, and not apprehending the weight, they grow rough and barren in language only. When their judgments are firm and out of danger, let them read both the old and the new; but no less take heed that their new flowers and sweetness do not as much corrupt as the others' dryness and squalor, if they do not choose carefully. Spenser, in affecting the ancients, writ no language; yet I would have him read for his matter, but as Virgil read Ennius. The reading of Homer and Virgil is counselled by Quintilian as the best way of informing youth and confirming man, for besides that the mind is raised with the height and sublimity of such a verse, it takes spirit from the greatness of the matter and is tincted with the best things. Tragic and lyric poetry is good too, and the comic with the best, if the manners of the reader be once in safety. In the Greek poets, as also in Plautus, we shall see the economy and disposition of poems better observed than in Terence and the later,[3] who thought the sole grace and virtue of their fable the sticking in of sentences, as ours do the forcing in of jests.

2. Of Diligence in Learning

We should not protect our sloth with the patronage of difficulty. It is a false quarel against nature that she helps understanding but in a few, when the most part of mankind are inclined by her thither if they would take the pains, no less than birds to fly, horses to run, etc.; which if they lose, it is through their own sluggishness, and by that means [they] become her prodigies, not her children. I confess nature in children is more patient of labour in study than in age, for the sense of the pain, the judgment of the labour is absent: they do not measure what they have done. And it is the thought and consideration that effects us, more than the weariness itself. Plato was not content with the learning that Athens could give him, but sailed into Italy for Pythagoras' knowledge; and yet not thinking himself sufficiently informed, went

3 Folio *latter*.

into Egypt to the priests and learned their mysteries. He laboured: so must we.

Many things may be learned together and performed in one point of time, as musicians exercise their memory, their voice, their fingers, and sometimes their head and feet at once. And so a preacher in the invention of matter, election of words, composition of gesture, look, pronunciation, motion, useth all these faculties at once. And if we can express this variety together, why should not diverse studies, at diverse hours, delight, when the variety is able alone to refresh and repair us; as when a man is weary of writing, to read, and then again of reading, to write? Wherein howsoever we do many things, yet are we, in a sort, still fresh to what we begin: we are recreated with change, as the stomach is with meats. But some will say this variety breeds confusion and makes that either we lose all or hold no more than the last. Why do we not then persuade husbandmen that they should not till land; help it with marl, lime, and compost; plant hop-gardens; prune trees; look to beehives; rear sheep and all other cattle at once? It is easier to do many things and continue, than to do one thing long.

It is not the passing through these learnings that hurt us, but the dwelling and sticking about them. To descend to those extreme anxieties and foolish cavils of grammarians is able to break a wit in pieces, being a work of manifold misery and vainness to be *elementarii senes.*[4] What a sight it is to see writers committed together by the ears for ceremonies, syllables, points, colons, commas, hyphens, and the like; fighting as for their fires and their altars, and angry that none are frighted at their noises and loud brayings under their asses' skins! There is hope of getting a fortune without digging in these quarries: *sed meliore in omne ingenio, animoque quam fortuna, sum usus.*[5] Yet even letters are, as it were, the bank of words, and restore themselves to an author as the pawns of language. But talking and eloquence are not the same: to speak and to speak well are two things: a fool may talk, but a

4 old men still at the elementary stage.
5 "but in all things I have found wit and spirit better than a fortune."

wise man speaks, and out of the observation, knowledge, and use of things. The reason why a poet is said he ought to have all knowledges, is that he should not be ignorant of the most, especially of those he will handle. And indeed, when the attaining of them is possible, it were a sluggish and base thing to despair. For frequent imitation of anything becomes a habit quickly. If a man should prosecute as much as could be said of everything, his work would find no end.

Ease and relaxation are profitable to all studies. The mind is like a bow, the stronger by being unbent. But the temper[6] in spirits is all when to command a man's wit, when to favour it. I have known a man vehement on both sides, that knew no mean, either to intermit his studies or call upon them again. When he hath set himself to writing, he would join night to day, press upon himself without release, not minding it till he fainted; and when he left off, resolve himself into all sports and looseness again, that it was almost a despair to draw him to his book; but once got to it, he grew stronger and more earnest by the ease. His whole powers were renewed; he would work out of himself what he desired, but with such excess as his study could not be ruled. He knew not how to dispose his own abilities or husband them; he was of that immoderate power against himself. Nor was he only a strong, but absolute speaker and writer; but his subtlety did not show itself – his judgment thought that a vice, for the ambush hurts more that is hid. He never forced his language, nor went out of the highway of speaking, but for some great necessity or apparent profit; for he denied figures to be invented for ornament, but for aid, and still thought it an extreme madness to bend or wrest that which ought to be right.[7] Many writers perplex their readers and hearers with mere nonsense: their writings need sunshine. Pure and neat language I love, yet plain and customary. A barbarous phrase hath often made me out of love with a good sense, and doubtful writing hath racked me beyond my patience.

6 due moderation
7 straight

I have known many excellent men that would speak suddenly, to the admiration of their hearers, who upon study and premeditation have been forsaken by their own wits, and no way answered their fame. Their eloquence was greater than their reading, and the things they uttered better than those they knew. Their fortune deserved better of them than their care. For men of present spirits, and of greater wits than study, do please more in the things they invent than in those they bring, and I have heard some of them compelled to speak, out of necessity, that have so infinitely exceeded themselves as it was better, both for them and their auditory, that they were so surprised, not prepared. Nor was it safe then to cross them, for their adversary, their anger, made them more eloquent. Yet these men I could not but love and admire that they returned to their studies. They left not diligence, as many do, when their rashness prospered. For diligence is a great aid, even to an indifferent wit, when we are not contented with the examples of our own age but would know the face of the former. Indeed the more we confer with, the more we profit by, if the persons be chosen.

3. Of Language in Oratory

Speech is the only benefit man hath to express his excellency of mind above other creatures: it is the instrument of society. Therefore Mercury, who is the president of language, is called *Deorum hominumque interpres.*[8] In all speech, words and sense are as the body and the soul. The sense is as the life and soul of language, without which all words are dead. Sense is wrought out of experience, the knowledge of human life and actions, or of the liberal arts, which the Greeks called *egkuklopaideian.* Words are the people's; yet there is a choice of them to be made. For *verborum delectus, origo est eloquentiae.*[9] They are to be chose according to the persons we make speak or the things we speak of. Some are of the camp, some of the council-board, some of the shop, some of the sheep-cote,

8 Go-between of gods and men.

9 "Delight in words is the beginning of eloquence": Vives.

some of the pulpit, some of the bar, etc. And herein is seen their elegance and propriety, when we use them fitly and draw them forth to their just strength and nature by way of translation[10] or metaphor. But in this translation we must only serve necessity *(Nam temere nihil transfertur a prudenti)*[11] or commodity, which is a kind of necessity: that is, when we either absolutely want a word to express by (and that is necessity), or when we have not so fit a word (and that is commodity): as when we avoid loss by it and escape obsceneness and gain in the grace and property which helps significance. Metaphors far-fetched hinder to be understood, and affected lose their grace: or when the person fetcheth his translations from a wrong place, as if a privy-counsellor should at the table take his metaphor from a dicing-house, or ordinary,[12] or a vintner's vault; or a justice of peace draw his similitudes from the mathematics; or a divine from a bawdy-house or taverns; or a gentleman of Northamptonshire, Warwickshire, or the Midland, should fetch all his illustrations to his country neighbours from shipping and tell them of the main-sheet and the bowline. Metaphors are thus many times deformed, as in him that said, *"Castratum morte Africani Rempublicam"*;[13] and another, *"stercus curiae Glauciam"*;[14] and *"cana nive conspuit Alpes"*.[15] All attempts that are new in this kind are dangerous and somewhat hard before they be softened with use. A man coins not a new word without some peril and less fruit; for if it happen to be received, the praise is but moderate; if refused, the scorn is assured. Yet we must adventure, for things at first hard and rough are by use made tender and gentle. It is an honest error that is committed following great chiefs.

Custom is the most certain mistress of language, as the public stamp makes the current money. But we must not be

10 figurative use
11 "Nothing is rashly translated by a prudent man."
12 eating-house
13 "The republic is mutilated by the death of Africanus."
14 "Glaucia, filth of the Senate-house."
15 "sprinkled the Alps with hoary snow."

too frequent with the mint, every day coining; nor fetch words from the extreme and utmost ages, since the chief virtue of style is perspicuity and nothing so vicious in it as to need an interpreter. Words borrowed of antiquity do lend a kind of majesty to style and are not without their delight sometimes, for they have the authority of years and out of their intermission do win to themselves a kind of grace like newness; but the eldest of the present and newest[16] of the past language is the best. For what was the ancient language, which some men so dote upon, but the ancient custom? Yet when I name custom, I understand not the vulgar custom, for that were a precept no less dangerous to language than life if we should speak or live after the manners of the vulgar; but that I call custom of speech which is the consent of the learned, as custom of life, which is the consent of the good. Virgil was most loving of antiquity, yet how rarely doth he insert *aquai* and *pictai!* [17] Lucretius is scabrous and rough in these; he seeks them as some do Chaucerisms with us, which were better expunged and banished. Some words are to be culled out for ornament and colour, as we gather flowers to strew houses or make garlands; but they are better when they grow to our style, as in a meadow where, though the mere grass and greenness delights, yet the variety of flowers doth heighten and beautify. Marry, we must not play or riot too much with them, as in *paronomasies;*[18] nor use too swelling or illsounding words, *quae per salebras, altaque saxa cadunt.*[19] It is true there is no sound but shall find some lovers, as the bitterest confections are grateful to some palates.

Our composition must be more accurate in the beginning and end than in the midst, and in the end more than in the beginning, for through the midst the stream bears us: and this is attained by custom more than care or diligence. We

16 Folio: *newness*
17 Archaic Latin forms.
18 Puns
19 "that pass over rough roads and great rocks": Martial, *Epig.* XI, 90.

must express readily and fully, not profusely; there is difference between a liberal and a prodigal hand. As it is a great point of art, when our matter requires it, to enlarge and veer out all sail, so to take it in and contract it is of no less praise when the argument doth ask it: either of them hath their fitness in the place. A good man always profits by his endeavour, by his help; yea, when he is dead, by his example and memory: so good authors in their style: a strict and succinct style is that where you can take away nothing without loss, and that loss to be manifest; the brief style is that which expresseth much in little; the concise style, which expresseth not enough, but leaves somewhat to be understood; the abrupt style, which hath many breaches, and doth not seem to end, but fall. The congruent and harmonious fitting of parts in a sentence hath almost the fastening and force of knitting and connection, as in stones well squared, which will rise strong a great way without mortar.

Periods are beautiful when they are not too long, for so they have their strength too, as in a pike or javelin. As we must take the care that our words and sense be clear, so if the obscurity happen through the hearers' or readers' want of understanding I am not to answer for them, no more than for their not listening or marking: I must neither find them ears nor mind. But a man cannot put a word so in sense but something about it will illustrate it, if the writer understand himself. For order helps much to perspicuity, as confusion hurts: *rectitudo lucem adfert; obliquitas et circumductio offuscat.*[20] We should therefore speak what we can the nearest way, so as we keep our gait, not leap; for too short may as well be not let into the memory as too long not kept in. Whatsoever loseth the grace and clearness converts into a riddle. The obscurity is marked but not the value: that perisheth and is past by, like the pearl in the fable. Our style should be like a skein of silk, to be carried and found by the

20 "Straightforwardness enlightens: obliqueness and circumlocution obscure"; Vives.

right thread, not ravelled and perplexed: then all is a knot, a heap.

There are words that do as much raise a style as others can depress it. Superlation[21] and overmuchness amplifies: it may be above faith, but never above a mean. It was ridiculous in Cestius when he said of Alexander: *"Fremit Oceanus, quasi indignetur, quod terras relinquas";*[22] but propitiously from Virgil:

Credas innare revulsas
Cyclades.[23]

He doth not say it was so, but seemed to be so: although it be somewhat incredible, that is excused before it be spoken. But there are hyperboles which will become one language that will by no means admit another, as: *nos esse P.R. exercitus, qui coelum possint perrumpere.*[24] Who would say this with us but a madman? Therefore we must consider in every tongue what is used, what received. Quintilian warns us that in no kind of translation or metaphor or allegory we must make a turn from what we began, as, if we fetch the original of our metaphor from sea and billows, we end not in flames and ashes: it is a most foul inconsequence. Neither must we draw out our allegory too long, lest either we make ourselves obscure or fall into affectation, which is childish. But why do men depart at all from the right and natural ways of speaking? Sometimes for necessity, when we are driven or think it fitter to speak that in obscure words or by circumstance which uttered plainly would offend the hearers; or to avoid obsceneness; or sometimes for pleasure and variety, as travellers turn out of the highway, drawn either by the commodity of a footpath or the delicacy or freshness of the fields. And all this is called figured language.

Language most shows a man: "speak that I may see thee."

21 exaggeration
22 "Ocean roars, as if angry at your leaving the land."
23 "You would think that the Cyclades, swept away, were swimming": *Aeneid*, VII, 691.
24 "that we are a Roman army which could break through to the stars": Caesar.

It springs out of the most retired and inmost parts of us, and is the image of the parent of it, the mind. No glass renders a man's form or likeness so true as his speech. Nay, it is likened to a man, and as we consider features and composition in a man, so words in language, in the greatness, aptness, sound, structure, and harmony of it. Some men are tall and big, so some language is high and great: then the words are chosen, their sound ample, the composition full, the absolution plenteous and poured out, all grave, sinewy, and strong. Some are little and dwarfs: so of speech, it is humble and low, the words poor and flat, the members and periods thin and weak, without knitting or number. The middle are of just stature: there the language is plain and pleasing, even, without stopping, round, without swelling; all well-turned, composed, elegant, and accurate. The vicious language is vast and gaping, swelling and irregular; when it contends to be high, full of rock, mountain, and pointedness; as it affects to be low, it is abject and creeps, full of bogs and holes. And according to their subject these styles vary and lose their names; for that which is high and lofty declaring excellent matter, becomes vast and tumorous speaking of petty and inferior things; so that which was even and apt in a mean and plain subject will appear most poor and humble in a high argument. Would you not laugh to meet a great counsellor of state in a flat cap, with his trunk-hose and a hobby-horse cloak, his gloves under his girdle, and yond haberdasher in a velvet gown furred with sable? There is a certain latitude in these things by which we find the degrees.

The next thing to the stature is the figure and feature in language, that is, whether it be round and straight, which consists of short and succinct periods, numerous and polished; or square and firm, which is to have equal and strong parts everywhere answerable and weighed. The third is the skin and coat, which rests in the well-joining, cementing, and coagmentation of words, whenas it is smooth, gentle, and sweet, like a table upon which you may run your finger without rubs and your nail cannot find a joint; not horrid rough, wrinkled, gaping, or chapped. After these the flesh and blood come in question. We say it is a fleshy style when there is much periphrasis and circuit of words, and when with more than enough it grows fat and corpulent, *arvina orationis,*[25] full of suet and tallow. It hath blood and juice when the words are proper and apt, their sound sweet, and the phrase neat and picked: *oratio uncta et bene pasta.*[26] But where there is redundancy, both the blood and juice are faulty and vicious: *redundat sanguine, quae multo plus dicit, quam necesse est.*[27] Juice in language is somewhat less than blood, for if the words be but becoming and signifying, and the sense gentle, there is juice; but where that wanteth the language is thin, flagging, poor, starved, scarce covering the bone, and shows like stones in a sack. Some men, to avoid redundancy, run into that, and while they strive to have no ill blood or juice they lose their good. There be some styles, again, that have not less blood, but less flesh and corpulence. These are bony and sinewy: *ossa habent et nervos.*[28]

In picture, light is required no less than shadow: so in style, height as well as humbleness. But beware they be not too humble, as Pliny pronounced of Regulus' writings: "You would think them written, not on a child, but by a child." Many out of their own obscene apprehensions refuse proper and fit words, as *occupy, nature,*[29] and the like. So the curious industry in some of having all alike good hath come nearer a vice than a virtue.

A man should so deliver himself to the nature of the subject whereof he speaks that his hearer may take knowledge of his discipline with some delight, and so apparel fair and good matter that the studious of elegancy be not defrauded; redeem arts from their rough and brakey[30] seats, where they lay hid

[25] "the fattiness of a speech."
[26] "a polished and well-conceived speech": Vives.
[27] "over-rich in blood, and saying more than is necessary": Vives.
[28] "they have bones and muscles."
[29] These words had secondary sexual meanings in Elizabethan English: *occupy:* cohabit; *nature:* discharge from the sexual organs.
[30] overgrown with briars or brushwood

and overgrown with thorns, to a pure, open and flowery light, where they may take the eye and be taken by the hand.

4. Of Judging Poets and Poetry

We have spoken sufficiently of oratory: let us now make a diversion to poetry. Poetry in the primogeniture had many peccant humours and is made to have more now, through the levity and inconstancy of men's judgments, whereas, indeed, it is the most prevailing eloquence and of the most exalted *charact.*[31] Now the discredits and disgraces are many it hath received through men's study[32] of depravation or calumny, their practice being to give it diminution of credit by lessening the professors' estimation and making the age afraid of their liberty; and the age is grown so tender of her fame as she calls all writings *aspersions.* That is the state-word, the phrase of court, Placentia College[33], which some call "Parasites' Place," the Inn of Ignorance.

Whilst I name no persons but deride follies, why should any man confess or betray himself? Why doth not that of St. Jerome come into their mind: *"Ubi generalis est de vitiis disputatio, ibi nullius esse personae injuriam"?*[34] Is it[35] such an inexpiable crime in poets to tax vices generally, and no offence in them who by their exception confess they have committed them particularly? Are we fallen into those times that we must not *Auriculas teneras mordaci rodere vero?*[36] *Remedii votum semper verius erat, quam spes.*[37] If men may by no means write freely or speak truth but when it offends not, why do physicians cure with sharp medicines or corrosives? Is not the same equally lawful in the cure of the mind that is in the cure of the body? Some vices, you will say, are

31 value
32 practice
33 A reference, perhaps, to the palace of the Farnese family at Piacenza, notorious as a breeding-place for pampered immorality and luxurious vice.
34 "Where censure is general, there is no injury to individuals."
35 Folio: *It is*
36 "gnaw tender ears with biting truth": Juvenal, *Pers.* Sat. I
37 "To pray for a cure was always more proper than to hope": Livy.

so foul that it is better they should be done than spoken. But they that take offence where no name, character, or signature doth blazon them seem to me like affected as women who, if they hear anything ill spoken of the ill of their sex, are presently moved as if the contumely respected their particular; and, on the contrary, when they hear good of good women, conclude that it belongs to them all. If I see anything that toucheth me, shall I come forth a betrayer of myself presently? No, if I be wise I'll dissemble it; if honest, I'll avoid it, lest I publish that on my own forehead which I saw there noted without a title. A man that is on the mending hand will either ingeniously confess or wisely dissemble his disease: and the wise and virtuous will never think anything belongs to themselves that is written, but rejoice that the good are warned not to be such, and the ill to leave to be such. The person offended hath no reason to be offended with the writer, but with himself; and so to declare that properly to belong to him which was so spoken of all men as it could be no man's several[38] but his that would wilfully and desperately claim it. It sufficeth I know what kind of persons I displease: men bred in the declining and decay of virtue, betrothed to their own vices, that have abandoned or prostituted their good names, hungry and ambitious of infamy, invested in all deformity, enthralled to ignorance and malice, of a hidden and concealed malignity, and that hold a concomitancy with evil.

There be some men are born only to suck out the poison of books, *habent venenum pro victu; imo, pro deliciis*[39] and such are they that only relish the obscene and foul things in poets — which makes the profession taxed. But by whom? Men that watch for it and, had they not had this hint, are so unjust valuers of letters as they think no learning good but what brings in gain. It shows they themselves would never have been of the professions they are but for the profits and fees. But if another learning, well used, can instruct to good

38 own
39 "To them poison is as a food — nay, as a delicacy."

life, inform manners, no less persuade and lead men than they threaten and compel, and have no reward, is it therefore the worse study? I could never think the study of wisdom confined only to the philosopher, or of piety[40] to the divine, or of state to the politic: but that he[41] which can feign a commonwealth, which is the poet, can govern it with counsels, strengthen it with laws, correct it with judgments, inform it with religion and morals, is all these. We do not require in him mere elocution, or an excellent faculty in verse, but the exact knowledge of all virtues and their contraries, with ability to render the one loved, the other hated, by his proper embattling them. The philosophers did insolently to challenge only to themselves that which the greatest Generals and gravest Councillors never durst: for such had rather do than promise the best things.

Nothing in our age, I have observed, is more preposterous than the running judgments upon poetry and poets, when we shall hear those things commended and cried up for the best writings which a man would scarce vouchsafe to wrap any wholesome drug in: he would never light his tobacco with them – and those men almost named for miracles who yet are so vile that if a man should go about to examine and correct them he must make all they have done but one blot. Their good is so entangled with their bad as forcibly one must draw on the other's death with it. A sponge dipped in ink will do all:

Comitetur punica librum
Spongia;[42]

and a little later:

Non possunt . . . . . multae, una litura potest.[43]

Yet their vices have not hurt them: nay, a great many they have profited, for they have been loved for nothing else. And

40 Gifford conj.: Folio reads *poetry*.
41 that man
42 "Let the book be accompanied by a Carthaginian sponge." Martial, *Epig.* IV, x.
43 "Many blots cannot [set my attempts at wit to rights], one blot may": Ibid.

this false opinion grows strong against the best men, if once it take root with the ignorant. Cestius[44] in his time, was preferred to Cicero, so far as the ignorant durst: they learned him without book, and had him often in their mouths. But a man cannot imagine that thing so foolish or rude but will find and enjoy an admirer, at least a reader or spectator. The puppets are seen now in despite of the players: Heath's epigrams[45] and the Sculler's poems[46] have their applause. There are never wanting that dare prefer the worst preachers, the worst pleaders, the worst poets: not that the better have left to write or speak better, but that they that hear them judge them worse: *Non illi pejus dicunt, sed hi corruptius judicant.*[47] Nay, if it were put to the question of the water-rhymer's works[48] against Spenser's, I doubt not but they would find more suffrages, because the most favour common vices, out of a prerogative the vulgar have to lose their judgments and like that which is naught.

Poetry, in this latter age, hath proved but a mean mistress to such as have wholly addicted themselves to her or given their names up to her family. They who have but saluted her on the by, and now and then tendered their visits, she hath done much for, and advanced in the way of their own professions (both the law and the gospel) beyond all they could have hoped or done for themselves without her favour. Wherein she doth emulate the time's grande[e]s, who accumulate all they can upon the parasite or freshman in their friendship, but think an old client or honest servant bound by his place to write and starve.

Indeed the multitude commend writers as they do fencers or wrestlers, who, if they come in robustiously and put for it with a deal of violence, are received for the braver fellows,

44 A street-orator in Rome who presumed to deliver replies to the orations of Cicero.
45 John Heath published his *Two Centuries of Epigrammes* in 1610.
46 John Taylor (1580-1653), a Thames waterman, wrote catchy popular verse.
47 "The former speak no worse, but the latter judge them by falser standards": Seneca Major.
48 Another reference to Taylor's poems.

when many times their own rudeness is a cause of their disgrace, and a slight touch of their adversary gives all that boisterous force the foil. But in these things the unskilful are naturally deceived, and judging wholly by the bulk think rude things greater than polished, and scattered more numerous than composed. Nor think this only to be true in the sordid multitude, but the neater[49] sort of our *gallants* – for all are the multitude; only they differ in clothes, not in judgment or understanding.

I remember the players have often mentioned it as an honour to Shakespeare that in his writing, whatsoever he penned, he never blotted out line.[50] My answer hath been, "Would he had blotted a thousand": which they thought a malevolent speech. I had not told posterity this, but for their ignorance, who choose that circumstance to commend their friend by wherein he most faulted, and to justify mine own candour, for I loved the man and do honour his memory (on this side idolatry) as much as any. He was, indeed, honest and of an open and free nature; had an excellent fancy, brave notions, and gentle expressions, wherein he flowed with that facility that sometime it was necessary he should be stopped: *"Sufflaminandus erat,"* [51] as Augustus said of Haterius. His wit was in his own power: would the rule of it had been so too. Many times he fell into those things could not escape laughter, as when he said, in the person of Caesar, one speaking to him: "Caesar thou dost me wrong." he replied: "Caesar did never wrong but with just cause," [52] and such like, which were ridiculous. But he redeemed his vices with his virtues. There was ever more in him to be praised than to be pardoned.

I do hear them say often, "Some men are not witty because they are not everywhere witty," than which nothing is more

49 more elegant

50 "We have scarce received from him a blot on his papers": Heminge and Condell, in the Preface to the 1st folio edition of Shakespeare's plays.

51 "He wanted checking."

52 Possibly referring to an early version of the lines in *Julius Caesar,* Act III: "Know Caesar doth not wrong, nor without cause will he be satisfied."

foolish. If an eye or a nose be an excellent part in the face, therefore be all eye or nose? I think the eyebrow, the forehead, the cheek, the chin, the lip, or any part else are as necessary and natural in the place. But now nothing is good that is natural: right and natural language seems to have least of the wit in it, that which is writhed and tortured is counted the more exquisite. Cloth of bodkin[53] or tissue must be embroidered, as if no face were fair that were not powdered or painted, no beauty to be had but in wresting and writhing our own tongue. Nothing is fashionable till it be deformed, and this is to write like a gentleman. All must be as affected and preposterous as our gallants' clothes, sweet bags,[54] and night-dressings, in which you would think our men lay-in, like ladies, it is so curious.[55]

5. Of Liberal Studies

Arts that respect the mind were ever reputed nobler than those that serve the body, though we less can be without them, as tillage, spinning, weaving, building, etc., without which we could scarce sustain life a day. But these were the works of every hand; the other of the brain only, and those the most generous and exalted wits and spirits, that cannot rest or acquiesce. The mind of man is still fed with labour: *opere pascitur.*[56]

There is a more secret cause, and the power of liberal studies lies more hid than it can be wrought out by profane wits. It is not every man's way to hit. They are men, I confess, that set the *charact*[57] and value upon things, as they love them; but science is not every man's mistress. It is as great a spite to be praised in the wrong place, and by the wrong person, as can be done to a noble nature.

I have ever observed it to have been the office of a wise patriot among the greatest affairs of the state to take care of

53 *baldaquin,* or *baudekin:* a rich brocade imported from Bagdad.
54 pomanders
55 fine
56 "It thrives on work."
57 worth

the commonwealth of learning. For schools, they are the seminaries of state, and nothing is worthier the study of a statesman than that part of the republic which we call the advancement of letters. Witness the care of Julius Caesar, who, in the heat of the civil war, writ his books of *Analogy*[58] and dedicated them to Tully. This made the late Lord St. Alban entitle his work *Novum Organum,* which though by the most of superficial men who cannot get beyond the title of *Nominals,* it is not penetrated or understood, it really openeth all defects of learning whatsoever, and is a book,

Qui longum noto scriptori porriget[59] *aevum.*[60]

My conceit of his person was never increased toward him by his place or honours, but I have, and do reverence him for the greatness that was only proper to himself, in that he seemed to me ever, by his work, one of the greatest men and most worthy of admiration that had been in many ages. In his adversity[61] I ever prayed that God would give him strength, for greatness he could not want. Neither could I condole in a word or syllable for him, as knowing no accident could do harm to virtue but rather help to make it manifest.

It was well noted[62] by the late Lord St. Alban that the study of words is the first distemper of learning, vain matter the second, and a third distemper is deceit or the likeness of truth, imposture held up by credulity. All these are the cobwebs of learning, and to let them grow in us is either sluttish or foolish. Nothing is more ridiculous than to make an author a dictator, as the schools have done Aristotle. The damage is infinite knowledge receives by it, for to many things a man owes but a temporary belief and a suspension of his own judgment, not an absolute resignation of himself or a perpetual captivity. Let Aristotle and others have their dues, but if we can make farther discoveries of truth and fitness than they,

58 Caesar's *De Analogia,* which has not survived, is said to have been written during a journey over the Alps.
59 Folio 1692: *proroget*
60 "which extends to eternity the fame of the writer": Horace.
61 at the time of his impeachment, trial and imprisonment.
62 In the *Advancement of Learning,* Book I.

why are we envied? Let us beware while we strive to add we do not diminish or deface: we may improve but not augment. By discrediting falsehood, truth grows in request. We must not go about like men anguished and perplexed for vicious affectations of praise, but calmly study the separation of opinions; find the errors have intervened, awake antiquity, call former times into question, but make no parties with the present; nor follow any fierce undertakers, mingle no matter of doubtful credit with the simplicity of truth, but gently stir the mould about the question, and avoid all digladiations,[63] facility of credit, or superstitious simplicity; seek the consonancy and concatenation of truth; stoop only to point of necessity and what leads to convenience. Then make exact animadversion where style hath degenerated, where flourished and thrived in choiceness of phrase and clean composition of sentence, sweet falling of the clause, varying an illustration by tropes and figures, weight of matter, worth of subject, soundness of argument, life of invention, and depth of judgment. This is *monte potiri,* to get to the hill: for no perfect discovery can be made upon a flat or a level.

I know nothing can conduce more to letters than to examine the writings of the ancients and not to rest in their sole authority or take all upon trust from them, provided the plagues of judging and pronouncing against them be away, such as are envy, bitterness, precipitation, impudence, and scurrile[64] scoffing. For to all the observations of the ancients we have our own experience, which, if we will use and apply, we have better means to pronounce. It is true, they opened the gates and made the way that went before us, but as guides, not commanders: *non domini nostri, sed duces fuere.*[65] Truth lies open to all: it is no man's several. *Patet omnibus veritas; nondum est occupata. Multum ex illa, etiam futuris relictum est.*[66]

63 sword-crossings
64 scurrilous
65 "They were not our masters, but our leaders."
66 "Truth is open to all: it has not yet been taken possession of. Much has come out of it, but still much remains for the future": Vives.

If in some things I dissent from others, whose wit, industry, diligence, and judgment I look up at and admire, let me not therefore hear presently of ingratitude and rashness. For I thank those that have taught me, and will ever, but yet dare not think the scope of their labour and enquiry was to envy their posterity what they also could add and find out. If I err, pardon me: *nulla ars simul et inventa est, et absoluta.*[67] I do not desire to be equal to those that went before, but to have my reason[s] examined with theirs, and so much faith to be given them or me as those shall evict. I am neither author nor fautor[68] of any sect. I will have no man addict himself to me, but if I have anything right, defend it as truth's, not mine save as it conduceth to a common good. It profits not me to have any man fence or fight for me, to flourish or take a side. Stand for truth and 'tis enough.

6. Of Writing Well

Now that I have informed you in the knowing these things, let me lead you by the hand a little farther in the direction of the use, and make you an able writer by practice. The conceits of the mind are pictures of things, and the tongue is the interpreter of those pictures. The order of God's creatures in themselves is not only admirable and glorious, but eloquent; then he who could apprehend the consequence of things in their truth and utter his apprehensions as truly were the best writer or speaker. Therefore Cicero said much when he said, *"Dicere recte nemo potest, nisi qui prudenter intelligit."* [69] The shame of speaking unskilfully were small, if the tongue only thereby were disgraced; but, as the image of a king in his seal ill-represented is not so much a blemish to the wax or the signet that sealed it, as to the prince it representeth, so disordered speech is not so much injury to the lips that give it forth, as to the disproportion and incoherence of things in themselves so negligently expressed. Neither can his mind be thought to be

67 "No art is at the same time discovered and perfected": Vives.
68 patron
69 "No one can speak well, who has not understood intelligently."

in tune whose words do jar; nor his reason in frame whose sentence is preposterous; nor his elocution clear and perfect whose utterance breaks itself into fragments and uncertainties. Were it not a dishonour to a mighty prince to have the majesty of his embassage spoiled by a careless ambassador, and is it not as great an indignity that an excellent conceit and capacity, by the indiligence of an idle tongue, should be disgraced? Negligent speech doth not only discredit the person of the speaker, but it discrediteth the opinion of his reason and judgment: it discrediteth the force and uniformity of the matter and substance. If it be so, then, in words, which fly and escape censure, and where one good phrase begs pardon for many incongruities and faults, how shall he, then, be thought wise whose penning is thin and shallow? How shall you look for wit from him whose leisure and head, assisted with the examination of his eyes, yield you no life or sharpness in his writing?

For a man to write well, there are required three necessaries: to read the best authors, observe the best speakers, and much exercise of his own style. In style to consider what ought to be written, and after what manner, he must first think and excogitate his matter, then choose his words and examine the weight of either. Then take care in placing and ranking both matter and words, that the composition be comely; and to do this with diligence and often. No matter how slow the style be at first so it be laboured and accurate: seek the best, and be not glad of the forward conceits or first words that offer themselves to us, but judge of what we invent and order what we approve. Repeat often what we have formerly written, which besides that it helps the consequence and makes the juncture better, it quickens the heat of imagination, that often cools in the time of setting down, and gives it new strength, as if it grew lustier by the going back: as we see in the contention of leaping, they jump farthest that fetch their race largest; or as in throwing a dart or javelin, we force back our arms to make our loose[70] the stronger. Yet if we have a fair gale of wind, I forbid not the steering out of our sail, so the favour of the gale deceive us not. For all that we invent doth please us in the conception or birth, else we would never set it down; but the safest is to return to our judgment and handle over again those things the easiness of which might make them justly suspected. So did the best writers in their beginnings: they imposed upon themselves care and industry; they did nothing rashly; they obtained first to write well and then custom made it easy and a habit. By little and little their matter showed itself to them more plentifully; their words answered; their composition followed; and all, as in a well-ordered family, presented itself in the place. So that the sum of all is: Ready writing makes not good writing, but good writing brings on ready writing. Yet when we think we have got the faculty, it is even then good to resist it, as to give a horse a check sometimes with [the] bit, which doth not so much stop his course as stir his mettle.

Again, whether a man's genius is best able to reach, thither it should more and more contend, lift and dilate itself, as men of low stature raise themselves on their toes, and so oft-times get even, if not eminent. Besides, as it is fit for grown and able writers to stand of themselves and work with their own strength, to trust and endeavour by their own faculties, so it is fit for the beginner and learner to study others, and the best. For the mind and memory are more sharply exercised in comprehending another man's things than our own, and such as accustom themselves, and are familiar with the best authors shall ever and anon find somewhat of them in themselves, and in the expression of their minds, even when they feel it not, be able to utter something like theirs which hath an authority above their own. Nay, sometimes it is the reward of a man's study, the praise of quoting another man fitly; and though a man be more prone and able for one kind of writing than another, yet he must exercise all, for as in an instrument,

70 release

so in style, there must be a harmony and concent of parts.

One, though he be excellent and the chief, is not to be imitated alone. For never no imitator ever grew up to his author: likeness is always on this side truth. Yet there happened in my time one noble speaker who was full of gravity in his speaking: his language, where he could spare or pass by a jest, was nobly censorious: no man ever spake more neatly, more pressly,[71] more weightily, or suffered less emptiness, less idleness in what he uttered. No member of his speech but consisted of the[72] own graces: his hearers could not cough or look aside from him without loss. He commanded where he spoke, and had his judges angry and pleased at his devotion:[73] no man had their affections more in his power: the fear of every man that heard him was lest he should make an end.

Cicero is said to be the only wit that the people of Rome had, equalled to their empire: *ingenium par imperio.*[74] We have had many, and in their several ages (to take in but the former *seculum*[75]): Sir Thomas More, the elder Wyatt, Henry Earl of Surrey, Chaloner,[76] Smith,[77] Elyot,[78] B[ishop]. Gardiner,[79] were for their times admirable, and the more because they began eloquence with us: Sir Nicho[las] Bacon was singular and almost alone in the beginning of Queen Elizabeth's times; Sir Philip Sidney and Mr. Hooker (in different matter) grew great masters of wit and language and in whom all vigour of invention and strength of judgment met; the Earl of Essex, noble and high; and Sir Walter Raleigh, not to be contemned either for judgment or style; Sir Henry Savile,[80]

71 Folio 1692: *prestly,* i.e. readily
72 Folio 1692: *his*
73 disposal
74 "talent equal to power"
75 century
76 Sir Thomas Chaloner (1521-1565), diplomatist, Latin poet, and translator.
77 Sir Thomas Smith (1513-1577), statesman, author of *De Republica Anglorum.*
78 Sir Thomas Elyot (1499-1546), author of the *Governour.*
79 Stephen Gardiner (1483-1555), Wolsey's secretary, classical scholar.
80 Sir Henry Savile (1549-1622), translator of Tacitus.

grave and truly lettered; Sir Edwin Sandys,[81] excellent in both; Lo[rd] Egerton,[82] the Chancellor, a grave and great orator, and best when he was provoked. But his learned and able successor is he who hath filled up all numbers, and performed that in our tongue which may be compared, or preferred, either to insolent Greece or haughty Rome. In short, within his view and about his times were all the wits born that could honour a language or help study. Now things daily fall: wits grow downward and eloquence grows backward. So that he may be named and stand as the mark and *acme*[83] of our language.

Wits made out their several expeditions then, for the discovery of truth, to find out great and profitable knowledges; had their several instruments for the disquisition of arts. Now there are certain *scioli*,[84] or smatterers, that are busy in the skirts and outsides of learning, and have scarce anything of solid literature to commend them. They may have some edging or trimming of a scholar, a welt or so, but it is no more. [Yet] I cannot think Nature is so spent and decayed that she can bring forth nothing worth her former years. She is always the same, like herself, and when she collects her strength is abler still. Men are decayed and studies: she is not.

I take this labour in teaching others that they should not be always to be taught, and I would bring my precepts into practice, for rules are ever of less force and value than experiments: yet with this purpose, rather to show the right way to those that come after than to detect any that have slipped before by error, and I hope it will be more profitable. For men do more willingly listen, and with more favour, to precept than reprehension. Among diverse opinions of an art, and most of them contrary in themselves, it is hard to make election, and therefore, though a man cannot invent new

81 Sir Edwin Sandys (1561-1629), statesman and author.
82 Sir Thomas Egerton (1540-1617), Lord Chancellor from 1603 to his death, when he was succeeded by Bacon.
83 supreme peak
84 charlatans

things after so many, he may do a welcome work yet to help posterity to judge rightly of the old. But arts and precepts avail nothing except nature be beneficial and aiding, and therefore these things are no more written to a dull disposition than rules of husbandry to a barren soil: no precepts will profit a fool, no more than beauty will the blind, or music the deaf.

As we should take care that our style in writing be neither dry nor empty, we should look again it be not winding or wanton with far-fetched descriptions. Either is a vice, but that is worse which proceeds out of want than that which riots out of plenty. The remedy of fruitfulness is easy, but no labour will help the contrary: I will like and praise some things in a young writer which yet if he continue in I cannot but justly hate him for the same. There is a time to be given all things for maturity; and that even your country husbandman can teach, who to a young plant will not put the pruning-knife, because it seems to fear the iron as not able to admit the scar. No more would I tell a green writer all his faults, lest I should make him grieve and faint and at last despair. For nothing doth more hurt than to make him so afraid of all things as he can endeavour nothing.

III. EXPLORATA

A Collection of Memorable Passages Derived From Many Sources

Fortuna.[1] Ill fortune never crushed that man whom good fortune deceived not. I therefore have counselled my friends never to trust to her fairer side, though she seemed to make peace with them, but to place all things she gave them so, as she might ask them again without their trouble; she might take them from them, not pull them; to keep always a distance between her and themselves. He knows not his own strength that hath not met adversity. Heaven prepares good men with crosses, but no ill can happen to a good man: contraries are not mixed. Yet that which happens to any man may to every man; but it is in his reason what he accounts it and will make it.

Change into extremity is very frequent and easy: as when a beggar suddenly grows rich he commonly becomes a prodigal, for to obscure his former obscurity he puts on riot and excess.

Consilia.[2] No man is so foolish but may give another good counsel sometimes, and no man is so wise but may easily err if he will take no other's counsel but his own. But very few men are wise by their own counsel, or learned by their own teaching: for he that was only taught by himself had a fool to his master.

Fama.[3] A fame that is wounded to the world would be better cured by another's *apology*[4] than its own, for few can apply medicines well themselves. Besides, the man that is once hated, both his good and his evil deeds oppress him: he is not easily emergent.

Negotia.[5] In great affairs it is a work of difficulty to please all, and oft-times we lose the occasion of carrying a business

1 Fortune
2 Advice
3 Reputation
4 justification
5 Affairs

well and thoroughly by our too much haste. For passions are spiritual rebels and raise sedition against the understanding.

Amor Patriae.[6] There is a necessity all men should love their country. He that professeth the contrary may be delighted with his words, but his heart is[7] there.

Ingenia.[8] Natures that are hardened to evil you shall sooner break than make straight. They are like poles that are crooked and dry: there is no attempting them.

Applausus.[9] We praise the things we hear with much more willingness than those we see, because we envy the present and reverence the past, thinking ourselves instructed by the one and overlaid by the other.

Opinio.[10] Opinion is a light, vain, crude, and imperfect thing, settled in the imagination but never arriving at the understanding, there to obtain the tincture of reason. We labour with it more than truth. There is much more holds us than presseth us. An ill fact is one thing, an ill fortune is another; yet both often-times sway us alike, by the error of our thinking.

Impostura.[11] Many men believe not themselves what they would persuade others, and less do the things which they would impose on others; but least of all know what they themselves most confidently boast. Only they set the sign of the cross over their outer doors, and sacrifice to their gut and their groin in their inner closets.

Iactura vitae.[12] What a deal of cold business doth a man mis-spend the better part of life in – in scattering compliments, tendering visits, gathering and venting news, following feasts and plays, making a little winter-love in a dark corner!

Honesta ambitio.[13] If divers men seek fame or honour by divers ways, so both be honest, neither is to be blamed; but

6 Patriotism
7 Swinburne conj. *not there*
8 Character
9 Praise
10 Conjecture
11 Deceit
12 Waste of life
13 Honourable ambition

they that seek immortality are not only worthy of leave, but of praise.

Impostorum fucus.[14] Imposture is a specious thing, yet never worse than when it feigns to be best, and to none discovered sooner than the simplest. For truth and goodness are plain and open, but imposture is ever ashamed of the light. A puppet-play must be shadowed and seen in the dark, for draw the curtain *et sordet gesticulatio.*[15]

Scitum Hispanicum.[16] It is a quick saying with the Spaniards: *Artes inter haeredes non dividi.*[17] Yet these have inherited their fathers' lying, and they brag of it. He is a narrow-minded man that affects a triumph in any glorious study: but to triumph in a lie, and a lie themselves have forged is frontless. Folly often goes beyond her bounds, but impudence knows none.

Vulgi expectatio.[18] Expectation of the vulgar is more drawn and held with newness than goodness. We see it in fencers, in players, in poets, in preachers, in all where fame promiseth anything; so it be new, though never so naught and depraved, they run to it and are taken. Which shows that the only decay or hurt of the best men's reputation with the people is their wits have outlived the people's palates. They have been too much, or too long a feast.

Claritas Patris.[19] Greatness of name in the father ofttimes helps not forth but overwhelms the son: they stand too near one another, the shadow kills the growth. So much that we see the grandchild come more and oftener to be the heir of the first than doth the second. He dies between: the possession is the third's.

Eloquentia.[20] Eloquence is a great and diverse thing, nor did she yet favour any man so much as to become wholly his.

14 The deceit of impostors
15 "and the gesticulations (of the puppets) are despised."
16 A Spanish proverb
17 "I have not left my arts to my heirs."
18 The interest of the mob
19 A father's fame. Folio: *patriae.*
20 Eloquence

He is happy that can arrive to any degree of her grace. Yet there are who prove themselves masters of her and absolute lords; but I believe they may mistake their evidence, for it is one thing to be eloquent in the schools, or in the hall, another at the bar, or in the pulpit. There is a difference between mooting[21] and pleading, between fencing and fighting. To make arguments in my study and confute them is easy, where I answer myself, not an adversary. So I can see whole volumes dispatched by the *umbratical*[22] doctors on all sides; but draw these forth into the just lists, let them appear *sub dio*,[23] and they are changed with the place; like bodies bred in the shade, they cannot suffer the sun or a shower, nor bear the open air: they scarce can find themselves, they that were wont to domineer so among their auditors. But indeed I would no more choose a rhetorician for reigning in a school, than I would a pilot for rowing in a pond.

Amor et odium.[24] Love that is ignorant and hatred have almost the same ends. Many foolish lovers wish the same to their friends which their enemies would: as to wish a friend banished, that they might accompany him in exile; or some great want, that they might relieve him; or a disease, that they might sit by him. They make a causeway to their courtesy by injury, as if it were not honester to do nothing than to seek a way to do good by a mischief.

Injuriae.[25] Injuries do not extinguish courtesies, they only suffer them not to appear fair. For a man that doth me an injury after a courtesy takes not away the courtesy but defaces it, as he that writes other verses upon my verses takes not away the first letters but hides them.

Beneficia.[26] Nothing is a courtesy unless it be meant us, and that friendly and lovingly. We owe no thanks to rivers that they carry our boats, or winds that they be favouring

21 raising a point for discussion
22 shade-frequenting; academic
23 in the open
24 Love and hatred
25 Injuries
26 Favours

and fill our sails, or meats that they be nourishing. For these are what they are necessarily. Horses carry us, trees shade us, but they know it not. It is true, some man may receive a courtesy and not know it; but never any man received it from him that knew it not. Many men have been cured of diseases by accidents; but they were not remedies. I myself have known one helped of an ague by falling into a water, another whipped out of a fever; but no man would ever use these for medicines. It is the mind, and not the event, that distinguisheth the courtesy from wrong. My adversary may offend the judge with his pride and impertinences and I win my cause; but he meant it not me as a courtesy. I escaped pirates by being shipwrecked: was the wreck a benefit therefore? No, the doing of courtesies aright is the mixing of the respects for his own sake and for mine. He that doth them merely for his own sake is like one that feeds his cattle to sell them: he hath his horse well dressed for Smithfield.[27]

Valor rerum.[28] The price of many things is far above what they are bought and sold for. Life and health, which are both inestimable, we have of the physician; as learning and knowledge, the true tillage of the mind, from our schoolmasters. But the fees of the one, or the salary of the other, never answer the value of what we received, but served to gratify their labours.

Memoria.[29] Memory, of all the powers of the mind, is the most delicate and frail: it is the first of our faculties that age invades. Seneca, the father, the rhetorician, confesseth of himself he had a miraculous one, not only to receive but to hold. I myself could, in my youth, have repeated all that ever I had made, and so continued till I was past forty. Since then it is much decayed in me, yet I can repeat whole books that I have read and poems of some selected friends which I have liked to charge my memory with. It was wont to be faithful

27 An open space outside the walls of London where horse and cattle markets were held
28 The value of things
29 Memory

to me, but shaken with age now and sloth, which weakens the strongest abilities, it may perform somewhat, but cannot promise much. By exercise it is to be made better and serviceable.

Whatsoever I pawned with it, while I was young and a boy, it offers me readily and without stops; but what I trust to it now, or have done of later years, it lays up more negligently and often-times loses, so that I receive mine own, though frequently called for, as if it were new and borrowed. Nor do I always find presently from it what I do seek, but while I am doing another thing, that I labour for will come; and what I sought with trouble will offer itself when I am quiet. Now in some men I have found it as happy as nature, who, whatsoever they read or pen, they can say without book presently, as if they did then write in their mind. And it is more wonder in such as have a swift style, for their memories are commonly slowest: such as torture their writings, and go into council for every word, must needs fix somewhat and make it their own at last, though but through their own vexation.

Comit. suffragia.[80] Suffrages in parliament are numbered, not weighed: nor can it be otherwise in those public councils, where nothing is so unequal as the equality, for there, how odd soever men's brains or wisdoms are, their power is always even and the same.

Stare a partibus.[81] Some actions, be they never so beautiful and generous, are often obscured by base and vile misconstructions, either out of envy or ill-nature, that judgeth of others as of itself. Nay, the times are so wholly grown to be either partial or malicious, that if he be a friend all sits well about him, his very vices shall be virtues; if an enemy, or of the contrary faction, nothing is good or tolerable in him; insomuch that we care not to discredit and shame our judgments to soothe our passions.

Deus in creaturis.[82] Man is read in his face; God in his

80 The votes of the assembly
81 Siding with political parties
82 God manifest in his creatures

creatures, but not as the philosopher, the creature of glory, reads him, but as the divine, the servant of humility. Yet even he must take care not to be too curious; for to utter truth of God, but as he thinks only, may be dangerous, Who is best known by our not knowing. Some things of him, so much as he hath revealed or commanded, it is not only lawful but necessary for us to know, for therein our ignorance was the first cause of our wickedness.

Veritas proprium hominis.[33] Truth is man's proper good, and the only immortal thing was given to our mortality to use. No good Christian or ethnic,[34] if he be honest, can miss it; no statesman or patriot should. For without truth all the actions of mankind are craft, malice, or what you will, rather than wisdom. Homer says[35] he hates him worse than hell-mouth that utters one thing with his tongue and keeps another in his breast: which high expression was grounded on divine reason. For a lying mouth is a stinking pit, and murders with the contagion it venteth. Besides, nothing is lasting that is feigned: it will have another face than it had, ere long: as Euripides saith, 'No lie ever grows old.'

Nullum vitium sine patrocinio.[36] It is strange there should be no vice without his patronage, that, when we have no other excuse, we will say we love it, we cannot forsake it; as if that made it not more a fault. We cannot, because we think we cannot; and we love it, because we will defend it. We will rather excuse it than be rid of it. That we cannot is pretended, but that we will not is the true reason. How many have I known that would not have their vices hid? Nay, and to be noted live like *antipodes* to others in the same city; never see the sun rise or set in so many years, but be as they were watching a corpse by torchlight; would not sin the common way, but held that a kind of rusticity: they would do it new or contrary, for the infamy. They were ambitious

33 Truth peculiar to Man
34 pagan
35 *Illiad,* IX, 313
36 No vice without its excuse

of living backward, and at last arrived at that, as they would love nothing but the vices, not the vicious customs. It was impossible to reform these natures; they were dried and hardened in their ill. They may say they desired to leave it, but do not trust them: and they may think they desired it, but they may lie for all that. They are a little angry with their follies, now and then: marry, they come into grace with them again quickly. They will confess they are offended with their manner of living—like enough, who is not? When they can put me in security that they are more than offended, that they hate it, then I'll harken to them and, perhaps, believe them: but many nowadays love and hate their ill together.

Ignorantia animae.[37] I know no disease of the soul but ignorance, not of the arts and sciences, but of itself. Yet relating to those it is a pernicious evil, the darkener of man's life, the disturber of his reason and common confounder of truth, with which a man goes groping in the dark no otherwise than if he were blind. Great understandings are most racked and troubled with it; nay, sometimes they will rather choose to die than not to know the things they study for. Think then what an evil it is, and what good the contrary.

Scientia.[38] Knowledge is the action of the soul and is perfect without the senses, as having the seeds of all science and virtue in itself; but not without the service of the senses: by those organs the soul works. She is a perpetual agent, prompt and subtle, but often flexible and erring, entangling herself like a silkworm. But her reason is a weapon with two edges, and cuts through. In her indagations[39] oft-times new scents put her by, and she takes in errors into her by the same conduits she doth truths.

De rebus mundanis.[40] If we would consider what our affairs are indeed, not what they are called, we should find

[37] The soul's ignorance
[38] Knowledge
[39] investigations
[40] On worldly affairs

more evils belong us than happen to us. How often doth that which was called a calamity prove the beginning and cause of a man's happiness? And on the contrary, that which happened or came to another with great gratulation and applause, how it hath lifted him but a step higher to his ruin, as if he stood before where he might fall safely.

Controvers. scriptores.[41] Some controverters in divinity are like swaggerers in a tavern, that catch that which stands next them, the candlestick or pots; turn everything into a weapon; oft-times they fight blindfold, and both beat the air. The one milks a he-goat; the other holds under a sieve. Their arguments are as fluxive as liquor spilt upon a table, which with your finger you may drain as you will. Such controversies or disputations, carried with more labour than profit, are odious, where most times the truth is lost in the midst or left untouched. And the fruit of their fight is that they spit one upon another and are both defiled. These fencers in religion I like not.

The body hath certain diseases that are with less evil tolerated than removed: as if to cure a leprosy a man should bathe himself with the warm blood of a murdered child. So in the Church some errors may be dissimuled with less inconvenience than can be discovered.

Iactantia intempestiva.[42] Men that talk of their own benefits are not believed to talk of them because they have done them, but to have done them because they might talk of them. That which had been great if another had reported it of them vanisheth and is nothing, if he that did it speak of it. For men, when they cannot destroy the deed, will yet be glad to take advantage of the boasting and lessen it.

Adulatio.[43] I have seen that poverty makes men do unfit things, but honest men should not do them: they should gain otherwise. Though a man be hungry, he should not play the

41 Writers at variance
42 Untimely boasting
43 Flattery

parasite. That hour wherein I would repent me to be honest, there were ways enow open for me to be rich. But flattery is a fine pick-lock of tender ears, especially of those whom fortune hath borne high upon their wings, that submit their dignity and authority to it by a soothing of themselves. For indeed men could never be taken in that abundance with the springes[44] of others' flattery if they began not there, if they did but remember how much more profitable the bitterness of truth were than all the honey distilling from a whorish voice, which is not praise but poison. But now it is come to that extreme folly, or rather madness, with some, that he that flatters them modestly or sparingly is thought to malign them. If their friend consent not to their vices, though he do not contradict them, he is nevertheless an enemy. When they do all things the worst way, even then they look for praise. Nay, they will hire fellows to flatter them with suits and suppers, and to prostitute their judgments. They have *livery-friends,* friends of the dish and of the spit, that wait their turns, as my Lord has his feasts and guests.

De vita humana.[45] I have considered our whole life is like a play wherein every man, forgetful of himself, is in travail with expression of another. Nay, we so insist in imitating others as we cannot, when it is necessary, return to ourselves; like children that imitate the vices of stammerers so long, till at last they become such, and make the habit to another nature, as it is never forgotten.

De piis et probis.[46] Good men are the stars, the planets of the ages wherein they live, and illustrate the times. God did never let them be wanting to the world: as Abel, for an example of innocency; Enoch, of purity; Noah, of trust in God's mercies; Abraham, of faith; and so of the rest. These, sensual men thought mad, because they would not be partakers or practisers of *their* madness. But they, placed high on the top of all virtue, looked down on the stage of the world and con-

44 snares
45 On human life
46 On good and upright men

temned the play of fortune: for though the most be players, some must be spectators.

Mores Aulici.[47] I have discovered that a feigned familiarity in great ones is a note of certain usurpation on the less. For great and popular men feign themselves to be servants to others to make those slaves to them. So the fisher provides baits for the trout, roach, dace, etc., that they may be food to him.

Divites.[48] He which is sole heir to many rich men, having besides his father's and uncles', the states of diverse his kindred come to him by accession, must needs be richer than father or grandfather. So they which are left heirs *ex asse*[49] of all their ancestors' vices, and by their good husbandry improve the old and daily purchase the new, must needs be wealthier in vice, and have a greater revenue or stock of ill to spend on.

Periculosa melancholia.[50] It is a dangerous thing when men's minds come to sojourn with their affections and their diseases eat into their strength, that when too much desire and greediness of vice hath made the body unfit or unprofitable it is yet gladded with the sight and spectacle of it in others, and for want of ability to be an actor is content to be a witness. It enjoys the pleasure of sinning in beholding others sin, as in dicing, drinking, drabbing, etc. Nay, when it cannot do all these it is offended with his own narrowness that excludes it from the universal delights of mankind, and oft-times dies of a melancholy that it cannot be vicious enough.

Falsae species fugiendae.[51] I am glad when I see any man avoid the infamy of a vice, but to shun the vice itself were better. Till he do that he is but like the prentice, who being loath to be spied by his master coming forth of Black Lucy's, went in again: to whom his master cried, "The more thou

47 The ways of princes
48 Wealthy men
49 as sole inheritors
50 Dangerous melancholy
51 False appearances must be shunned

runnest that way to hide thyself, the more thou art in the place." So are those that keep a tavern all day that they may not be seen at night. I have known lawyers, divines, yea, great ones, of this heresy.

Decipimur specie.[52] There is a greater reverence had of things remote or strange to us than of much better, if they be nearer and fall under our sense. Men, and almost all sorts of creatures, have their reputation by distance. Rivers, the farther they run and more from their spring, the broader they are and greater. And where our original is known we are the less confident: among strangers we trust fortune. Yet a man may live as renowned at home, in his own country, or a private village, as in the whole world. For it is virtue that gives glory. That will endenizon a man everywhere. It is only that can naturalise him. A native, if he be vicious, deserves to be a stranger and cast out of the commonwealth as an alien.

Dejectio aulic.[53] A dejected countenance and mean clothes beget often a contempt ,but it is with the shallowest creatures – courtiers, commonly. Look up even with them in a new suit, you get above 'em straight. Nothing is more short-lived than pride: it is but while their clothes last. Stay but while these are worn out, you cannot wish the thing more wretched or dejected.

Hypocrita.[54] *Puritanus Hypocrita est Haereticus, quem opinio propriae perspicaciae, qua sibi videtur, cum paucis, in Ecclesiae dogmatibus errores quosdam animadvertisse, de statu mentis deturbavit: unde sacro furore percitus, phrenetice pugnat contra Magistratus, sic ratus, obedientiam praestare Deo.*[55]

52 Appearances deceive
53 The courtier brought low
54 Hypocrisy
55 "The Puritan is a heretical hypocrite, insane through conceit of his own perspicacity, by means of which, so he supposes, he has, along with a few others, discovered errors in the dogma of the Church: and so, inspired by sacred wrath, he fights against the authorities in the belief that he is acting in obedience to God."

IV. OF STATECRAFT

Wise, is rather the attribute of a Prince, than *learned,* or *good.* The learned man profits others rather than himself: the good man, rather himself than others: but the Prince commands others, and doth himself. The wise Lycurgus[1] gave no law but what himself kept. Sulla[2] and Lysander[3] did not so: the one, living extremely dissolute himself, enforced frugality by the laws: the other permitted those licenses to others which himself abstained from. But the Prince's prudence is his chief art, and safety. In his counsels and deliberations he foresees the future times. In the equity of his judgment he hath remembrance of the past, and knowledge of what is to be done or avoided for the present. Hence the Persians gave out their Cyrus[4] to have been nursed by a bitch, a creature to encounter ill, as of sagacity to seek out good: showing that wisdom may accompany fortitude, or it leaves to be and puts on the name of *rashness.*

A Prince without Letters is a pilot without eyes. All his government is groping. In sovereignty, it is a most happy thing not to be compelled; but so it is the most miserable not to be counselled. And how can he be counselled that cannot see to read the best counsellors, which are books, for they neither flatter us nor hide from us? He may hear, you will say. But how shall he always be sure to hear truth, or be counselled the best things, not the sweetest? They say Princes learn no art truly, but the art of horsemanship. The reason is, the brave beast is no flatterer. He will throw a Prince as soon as his groom. Which is an argument that the good counsellors to Princes are the best instruments of a good age. For though the Prince himself be of most prompt inclination to all virtue, yet the best pilots have need of mariners, besides sails, anchor, and other tackle.

1 Legendary reformer and law-giver of Sparta
2 Roman dictator of the 2nd century B.C.
3 Spartan ruler in the 4th century B.C. who was deposed for misgovernment
4 King of Persia in the 6th century B.C.

There is a great difference in the understanding of some Princes, as in the quality of their ministers about them. Some would dress their masters in gold, pearl, and all true jewels of Majesty, others furnish them with feathers, bells and ribbands, and are therefore esteemed the fitter servants. But they are ever good men that must make good the times: if the men be naught, the times will be such. *Finis expectandus est in unoquoque hominum: animali, ad mutationem promptissimo.*[5]

When a virtuous man is raised it brings gladness to his friends, grief to his enemies, and glory to his posterity. Nay, his honours are a great part of the honour of the times, when by this means he is grown to active men an example, to the slothful a spur, to the envious a punishment.

Learning needs rest: Sovereignty gives it. Sovereignty needs counsel: Learning affords it. There is such a consociation of offices between the Prince and whom his favour breeds, that they may help to sustain his power as he their knowledge. It is the greatest part of his liberality, his favour; and from whom doth he hear discipline more willingly, or the arts discoursed more gladly, than from those whom his own bounty and benefits have made able and faithful?

In being able to counsel others, a man must be furnished with an universal store in himself to the knowledge of all Nature. That is the matter and seed-plot: there are the seats of all argument and invention. But especially you must be cunning in the nature of man. There is the variety of things, which are as the elements and letters which his art and wisdom must rank and order to the present occasion. For we see not all letters in single words, nor all places in particular discourses. That cause seldom happens wherein a man will use all arguments.

The two chief things that give a man reputation in counsel are the opinion of his honesty and the opinion of his wisdom. The authority of those two will persuade when the same coun-

5 "Every man must expect to die: for man is an animal most prone to change."

sels, uttered by other persons less qualified, are of no efficacy or working. Wisdom without honesty is mere craft and cosenage,[6] and therefore the reputation of honesty must first be gotten, which cannot be but by living well. A good life is a main argument. Next a good life, to beget love in the persons we counsel by dissembling our knowledge of ability in ourselves and avoiding all suspicion of arrogance, ascribing all to their instruction, as an ambassador to his master, or a subject to his sovereign, seasoning all with humanity and sweetness, only expressing care and solicitude. And not to counsel rashly, or on the sudden, but with advice and meditation *(Dat nox consilium)*.[7] For many foolish things fall from wise men if they speak in haste or be extemporal. It therefore behooves the giver of counsel to be circumspect, especially to beware of those with whom he is not thoroughly acquainted, lest any spice of rashness, folly, or self-love appear, which will be marked by new persons and men of experience in affairs.

And to the Prince, or his Superior, to behave himself modestly and with respect, yet free from flattery or empire; not with insolence or precept, but as the Prince were already furnished with the parts he should have, especially in affairs of state. For in other things they will more easily suffer themselves to be taught or reprehended: they will not willingly contend, but hear, with Alexander, the answer the musician gave him: *Absit, o Rex, ut tu melius haec scias quam ego.*[8]

I have marked among the nobility, some are so addicted to the service of the Prince and Commonwealth as they look not for spoil: such are to be honoured and loved. There are others which no obligation will fasten on, and they are of two sorts. The first are such as love their own ease, or out of vice of nature or self-direction avoid business and care: yet these the Prince may use with safety. The other remove themselves upon craft, and design (as the architects say), with a premeditated thought to their own rather than their Prince's profit:

6 deceit
7 "Night brings counsel."
8 "Let it not be, Sire, that you know this better than I": Plutarch.

such let the Prince take heed of and not doubt to reckon in the list of his open enemies. The great thieves of a state are lightly the officers of the Crown: they hang the less still, play the pikes in the pond, eat whom they list. The net was never spread for the hawk or buzzard that hurt us, but the harmless birds they are good meat.

Dat veniam corvis, vexat censura columbas:[9]

Non rete accipitri tenditur, neque miluo.[10]

But they are not always safe, though, especially when they meet with wise masters. They can take down all the huff and swelling of their looks, and like dexterous auditors place the counter where he shall value nothing. Let them but remember Lewis the eleventh,[11] who, to a Clerk of the Exchequer that came to be Lord Treasurer, and had for his device represented himself sitting upon Fortune's wheel, told him he might do well to fasten it with a good strong nail, lest, turning about, it might bring him where he was again. As indeed it did.

The vulgar are commonly ill-natured, and always grudging against their governors, which makes that a Prince has more business and trouble with them than ever Hercules had with the bull, or any other beast, by how much they have more heads than will be reined with one bridle. There was not that variety of beasts in the Ark as is of beastly natures in the multitude, especially when they come to that iniquity to censure their sovereign's actions. Then all the counsels are made good or bad by the events. And it falleth out that the same facts receive from them the names, now of diligence, now of vanity, now of majesty, now of fury, where they ought wholly to hang on his mouth, as he to consist of himself, and not others' counsels.

After God, nothing is to be loved of man like the Prince. He violates nature that doth it not with his whole heart: for when he hath put on the care of the public good and com-

9 "He pardons the crows, but censures the doves": Juvenal, *Sat.* II, 63.
10 "No net is stretched for the hawk or the kite": Terence, *Phormio*, II, ii.
11 Louis XI (1423-1483), King of France

mon safety, I am a wretch, and put off man, if I do not reverence and honour him in whose charge all things divine and human are placed.

There is a great variation between him that is raised to the sovereignty by the favour of his peers and him that comes to it by the suffrage of the people. The first holds with more difficulty, because he hath to do with many that think themselves his equals and raised him for their own greatness and oppression of the rest. The latter hath no upbraiders, but was raised by them that sought to be defended from oppression, whose end is both the easier and the honester to satisfy. Besides, while he hath the people to friend, who are a multitude, he hath the less fear of the nobility, who are but few. Nor let the common proverb of "He that builds on the people, builds on the dirt" discredit my opinion. For that hath only place where an ambitious and private person for some popular end trusts in them against the public Justice and Magistrate. There they will leave him. But when a Prince governs them so as they have still need of his administration (for that is his art), he shall ever make and hold them faithful.

A Prince should exercise his cruelty, not by himself but by his ministers, so he may save himself and his dignity with his people by sacrificing those when he list, saith the great Doctor of State, Machiavelli.[12] But I say, he puts off man and goes into a beast that is cruel. No virtue is a Prince's own, or becomes him more than clemency, and no glory is greater than to be able to save with his power. Many punishments sometimes, and in some cases, as much discredit a Prince as many funerals a physician. The state of things is secured by clemency: severity represseth a few, but it irritates more. The lopping of trees makes the boughs shoot out thicker, and the taking away of some kind of enemies increaseth the number. It is then most gracious in a Prince to pardon when many about would make him cruel; to think then how much he can save, when others tell him how much he can destroy; not to con-

12 Machiavelli's *Il Principe* (1513) was a favorite subject for refutation by pamphleteers and satirists

sider what the impotence of others hath demolished, but what his own greatness can sustain. These are a Prince's virtues, and they that give him other counsels are but the hangman's factors.

He is the arbiter of life and death: when he finds no other subject for his mercy, he should spare himself. All his punishments are rather to correct than to destroy. Why are prayers with Orpheus[13] said to be the daughters of Jupiter, but that Princes are thereby admonished that the petitions of the wretched ought to have more weight with them than the Laws themselves? It was a great accu[mu]lation to his Majesty's deserved praise that men might openly visit and pity those whom his greatest prisons had at any time received, or his laws condemned.

He that is cruel to halves, saith the said St. Nicolas,[14] loseth no less the opportunity of his cruelty than of his benefits, for then to use his cruelty is too late, and to use his favours will be interpreted fear and necessity, and so he loseth the thanks. Still the counsel is cruelty. But Princes, by hearkening to cruel counsels, become in time obnoxious to the authors, their flatterers and ministers, and are brought to that, that when they would, they dare not change them: they must go on and defend cruelty with cruelty: they cannot alter the habit. It is then grown necessary they must be as ill as those have made them, and in the end they will grow more hateful to themselves than to their subjects. Whereas, on the contrary, the merciful Prince is safe in love, not in fear. He needs no emissaries, spies, intelligencers, to entrap true subjects. He fears no libels, no treasons. His people speak what they think, and talk openly what they do in secret: they have nothing in their breasts that they need a cipher for. He is guarded with his own benefits.

13 Orpheus was regarded as the founder of the mystic cult of Orphism, which flourished in Greece in the 6th century B.C.
14 Niccolo Machiavelli

The strength of Empire is in religion. What else is the Palladium,[15] with Homer, that kept Troy so long from sacking? Nothing more commends the sovereign to the subject than it. For he that is religious must be merciful and just necessarily, and they are two strong ties upon mankind. Justice is the virtue that innocence rejoiceth in. Yet even that is not always so safe but it may love to stand in the sight of mercy, for sometimes misfortune is made a crime, and then innocence is succoured, no less than virtue. Nay, oftentimes virtue is made capital, and through the condition of the times it may happen that that may be punished with our praise. Let no man therefore murmur at the actions of the Prince, who is placed so far above him. If he offend, he hath his discoverer. God hath a height beyond him. But where the Prince is good, Euripides saith, "God is a Guest in a human body."

The complaint of Caligula was most wicked, of the condition of his times, when he said they were not famous by any public calamity, as the reign of Augustus was by the defeat of Varus and the legions, and that of Tiberius by the falling of the theatre at Fidenae,[16] whilst his oblivion was imminent through the prosperity of his affairs: as that other voice of his was worthier a headsman than a head, when he wished the people of Rome had but one neck. But he found, when he fell, they had many hands. A tyrant, how great and mighty soever he may seem to cowards and sluggards, is but one creature, one animal.

There is nothing with some Princes sacred above their majesty, or prophane but what violates their sceptres. But a Prince, with such counsel is like the god Terminus,[17] of stone, his own landmark; or, as it is in the fable, a crowned lion. It is dangerous offending such an one, who, being angry, knows not how to forgive, that cares not to do anything, for

[15] The ancient image of Pallas on which, according to Homer, the safety of Troy depended. It was captured by Diomedes before the fall of the city.
[16] An ancient town five miles north of Rome
[17] The sacred boundary-stone in the temple of the Capitoline Jupiter at Rome

maintaining or enlarging of empire, kills not men, or subjects, but destroyeth whole countries, armies, mankind, male and female, guilty or not guilty, holy or prophane, yea, some that have not seen the light. All is under the law of their spoil and license. But the Princes that neglect their proper office thus, their fortune is often-times to draw a Sejanus[18] to be near about 'em, who will at last affect to get above 'em,[19] and put them in a worthy fear of rooting both them out and their family. For no men hate an evil Prince more than they that helped to make him such: and none more boastingly weep his ruin than they that procured and practiced it. The same path leads to ruin which did to rule, when men profess a license in governing. A good king is a public servant.

If men did know what shining fetters, gilded miseries, and painted happiness thrones and sceptres were, there would not be so frequent strife about the getting or holding of them. There would be more principalities than princes. For a Prince is the pastor of the people. He ought to shear, no[t] to flay his sheep: to take their fleeces, not their fells. Who were his enemies before, being a private man, become his children now he is public. He is the soul of the commonwealth, and ought to cherish it as his own body. Alexander the Great was wont to say, he hated that gardener that plucked his herbs or flowers up by the roots. A man may milk a beast till the blood come: churn milk and it yieldeth butter, but wring the nose and the blood followeth. He is an ill Prince that so pulls his subjects' feathers as he would not have them grow again, that makes his exchequer a receipt for the spoils of those he governs. No: let him keep his own, not affect his subjects'; strive rather to be called just than powerful; not, like the Roman tyrants, affect the surnames[20] that grow by human slaughters; neither to seek war in peace, or peace in war; but to observe faith given, though to an enemy; study piety

18 Confidant of the Emperor Tiberius who plotted to supplant him.
19 Folo: *about him . . . above him*
20 the honorific titles accorded to rulers and generals, to celebrate their conquests

towards the subject; show care to defend him; be slow to punish in diverse cases, but be a sharp and severe revenger of open crimes; break no decrees, or dissolve no orders, to slacken the strength of the laws; choose neither magistrates civil or ecclesiastic by favour or price, but by long disquisition and report of their worth, by all suffrages; sell no honours, nor give them hastily, but bestow them with counsel and for reward — if he do, acknowledge it, though late, and mend it, for princes are easy to be deceived, and what wisdom can escape it where so many court-arts are studied?

But above all, the Prince is to remember that when the great day of account comes, which neither magistrate nor prince can shun, there will be a reckoning for those whom he hath trusted as for himself, which he must provide. And if piety be wanting in the priests, equity in the judges, or the magistrate be found rated at a price, what justice or religion is to be expected, which are the only two attributes make kings akin to gods, and is the Delphic sword, both to kill sacrifices and to chastise offenders?

V. THE ART OF POETRY

Observations on the Theory of Poetry, for Fuller Expansion and Comment

What is a poet?

A poet is that which by the Greeks is called *kat' exochen ho poietes,*[1] a maker, or a feigner: his art, an art of imitation or feigning, expressing the life of man in fit measure, numbers, and harmony; according to Aristotle from the word *poiein,* which signifies to make or feign. Hence he is called a poet, not he which writeth in measure only, but that feigneth and formeth a fable and writes things like the truth. For the fable and fiction is, as it were, the form and soul of any poetical work, or poem.

What mean you by a poem?

A poem is not alone any work or composition of the poet's in many or few verses, but even one alone verse sometimes makes a perfect poem: as when Aeneas hangs up and consecrates the arms of Abas, with the inscription:

Aeneas haec de Danais victoribus arma,[2]

and calls it a poem, or *carmen.* Such are those in Martial:

Omnia, Castor, emis: sic fiet, ut omnia vendas[3]

and:

Pauper videri Cinna vult, et est pauper.[4]

So were Horace his odes called *carmina,* his lyric songs. And Lucretius designs a whole book, in his sixth:

Quod in primo quoque carmine claret.[5]

And anciently all the oracles were called *carmina;* or whatever sentence was expressed, were it much or little, it was called an epic, dramatic, lyric, elegiac, or epigrammatic poem.

But how differs a poem from what we call poesy?

1 "The man who makes outstandingly."
2 "Aeneas, these arms from Trojan victories": Virgil, *Aeneid* III.
3 "You buy everything, Castor, and so you will come to sell everything." Martial, *Epig.* VIII, 19.
4 "Cinna wants to appear a poor man — and is a poor man."
5 "which is clear in the first book also."

A poem, as I have told you, is the work of the poet, the end and fruit of his labour and study. Poesy is his skill or craft of making, the very fiction itself, the reason or form of the work. And these three voices differ, as the thing done, the doing, and the doer; the thing feigned, the feigning, and the feigner: so the poem, the poesy, and the poet. Now, the poesy is the habit or the art, nay, rather the queen of arts, which had her original from heaven, received thence from the Hebrews, and had in prime estimation with the Greeks, transmitted to the Latin and all nations that professed civility. The study of it, if we will trust Aristotle, offers to mankind a certain rule and pattern of living well and happily, disposing us to all civil offices of society. If we will believe Tully, it nourisheth and instructeth our youth, delights our age, adorns our prosperity, comforts our adversity, entertains us at home, keeps us company abroad, travails with us, watches, divides the times of our earnest and sports, shares in our country recesses and recreations, insomuch as the wisest and best learned have thought her the absolute mistress of manners and nearest of kin to virtue. And whereas they entitle philosophy to be a rigid and austere poesy, they have, on the contrary, styled poesy a dulcet and gentle philosophy, which leads on and guides us by hand to action, with a ravishing delight and incredible sweetness.

But, before we handle the kinds of poems, with their special differences, or make court to the art itself, as a mistress, I would lead you to the knowledge of our poet by a perfect information what he is, or should be by nature, by exercise, by imitation, by study; and so bring him down through the discipline of grammar, logic, rhetoric, and the ethics, adding somewhat out of all peculiar to himself and worthy of your admittance or reception.

First, we require in our poet, or maker[6] (for that title our language affords him elegantly, with the Greeks), a goodness

[6] Jonson's requirements for a poet are suggested by Sidney in the *Apologie for Poetrie.*

of natural wit: for, whereas all other arts consist of doctrine and precepts, the poet must be able by nature and instinct to pour out the treasure of his mind, and, as Seneca saith, *"Aliquando secundus Anacreontem insanire, jucundum esse,"* [7] by which he understands the poetical rapture; and according to that of Plato, *'Frustra poeticus fores sui compos pulsavit";*[8] and of Aristotle, *"Nullum magnum ingenium sine mixtura dementiae fuit. Nec potest grande aliquid, et supra caeteros loqui, nisi mota mens."* [9] Then it riseth higher, as by a divine instinct, when it contemns common and known conceptions. It utters somewhat above a mortal mouth. Then it gets aloft and flies away with its rider, whither before it was doubtful to ascend. This the poets understood by their Helicon, Pegasus, or Parnassus, and this made Ovid to boast:

Est Deus in nobis; agitante calescimus illo:
Sedibus aethereis spiritus ille venit;[10]

and Lipsius to affirm: *"Scio, poetam neminem praestantem fuisse, sine parte quadam uberiore divinae aurae."* [11] And hence it is that the coming up of good poets (for I mind not mediocres, or *imos)*[12] is so thin and rare among us: every beggarly corporation affords the state a major, or two bailiffs, yearly, but *solus rex aut poeta non quotannis nascitur.*[13]

To this perfection of nature in our poet we require exercise of those parts, and frequent. If his wit will not arrive suddenly at the dignity of the ancients, let him not yet fall out with it, quarrel, or be over-hastily angry, offer to turn it away from study in a humour; but come to it again upon better cogitation, try another time with labour. If then it succeed not, cast not away the quills yet, nor scratch the wainscot; beat not

7 "It is pleasant, according to Anacreon, to be frenzied at times."
8 "Master of himself, he beat in vain on the doors of poetry."
9 "No great genius existed without an element of madness. It is not possible to say a great or noble thing unless the spirit is moved."
10 "There is a god within us, and we glow when he stirs us: the inspiration comes from heaven."
11 "I know that no poet was great without a rich share of divine inspiration."
12 the downright bad
13 "It is only a king or a poet that is not born every year": Petronius.

the poor desk, but bring all to the forge and file again, turn it anew. There is no statute law of the kingdom bids you be a poet against your will, or the first quarter. If it come in a year or two, it is well. The common rhymers pour forth verses, such as they are, extempore, but there never come[s] from them one sense worth the life of a day. A rhymer and a poet are two things. It is said of the incomparable Virgil that he brought forth his verses like a bear, and after formed them with licking. Scaliger, the father, writes it of him that he made a quantity of verses in the morning, which before night he reduced to a less number. But that which Valerius Maximus hath left recorded of Euripides, the tragic poet, his answer to Alcestis, another poet, is as memorable as modest: who, when it was told to Alcestis that Euripides had in three days brought forth but three verses, and those with some difficulty and throes, Alcestis glorying he could with ease have sent forth a hundred in the space, Euripides roundly replied, "Like enough. But here is the difference: thy verses will not last those three days; mine will to all time." Which was as to tell him he could not write a verse. I have met many of these rattles that made a noise and buzzed. They had their hum, and no more. Indeed, things wrote with labour deserve to be so read, and will last their age.

The third requisite in our poet, or maker, is imitation: to be able to convert the substance or riches of another poet to his own use: to make choice of one excellent man above the rest, and so to follow him till he grow very he, or so like him as the copy may be mistaken for the principal – not as a creature that swallows what it takes in crude, raw, or undigested, but that feeds with an appetite, and hath a stomach to concoct, divide, and turn all into nourishment; not to imitate servilely, as Horace saith, and catch at vices for virtue, but to draw forth out of the best and choicest flowers with the bee, and turn all into honey, work it into one relish and savour, make our imitation sweet, observe how the best writers have imitated, and follow them: how Virgil and Statius have imitated Homer; how Horace, Archilochus;[14] how Alcaeus[15] and the other lyrics; and so of all the rest.

But that which we especially require in him is an exactness of study and multiplicity of reading, which maketh a full man, not alone enabling him to know the history or argument of a poem and to report it, but so to master the matter and style as to show he knows how to handle, place, or dispose of either with elegancy, when need shall be: and not think he can leap forth suddenly a poet by dreaming he hath been in Parnassus, or having washed his lips, as they say, in Helicon. There goes more to his making than so. For to nature, exercise, imitation, and study, art must be added to make all these perfect. And though these challenge to themselves much in the making up of our maker, it is art only can lead him to perfection and leave him there in possession, as planted by her hand. It is the assertion of Tully: "If to an excellent nature there happen an accession or conformation of learning and discipline, there will then remain somewhat noble and singular." For, as Simylus[16] said in Stobaeus:[17]

oute phusis hikane ginetai technes ater
oute pan techne me phusin kektemene[18]

without art, nature can never be perfect; and without nature, art can claim no being. But our poet must beware that his study be not only to learn of himself, for he that shall affect to do that confesseth his ever having a fool to his master. He must read many, but ever the best and choicest: those that can teach him anything he must ever account his masters and reverence, among whom Horace, and he that taught him, Aristotle, deserve to be the first in estimation. Aristotle was the first accurate critic, and truest judge, nay, the greatest philosopher the world ever had, for he noted the vices of all knowledges, in all creatures, and out of many men's perfec-

14 Greek poet of the 7th century B.C.
15 Greek lyric poet of the 7th-6th centuries B.C.
16 Greek writer of comedy of the 4th century B.C. of whom little is known
17 Greek anthologist of the 6th century B.C. Folio: *Stobus*
18 "Nature is wanting without art; and art, without nature": Stobaeus, *Florilegium*, II.

tions in a science he formed still one art. So he taught us two offices together: how we ought to judge rightly of others, and what we ought to imitate specially in ourselves. But all this in vain, without a natural wit and a poetical nature in chief; for no man so soon as he knows this or reads it shall be able to write the better, but as he is adapted to it by nature, he shall grow the perfecter writer. He must have civil prudence and eloquence; and that whole, not taken up by snatches or pieces, in sentences or remnants, when he will handle business or carry councils, as if he came then out of the declaimers' gallery or shadow,[19] but furnished out of the body of the state, which commonly is the school of men.

The poet is the nearest borderer upon the orator, and expresseth all his virtues, though he be tied more to numbers: is his equal in ornament and above him in his strengths. And of the kind, the comic comes nearest, because, in moving the minds of men and stirring of affections, in which oratory shows and especially approves her eminence, he chiefly excels. What figure of a body was Lysippus ever able to form with his graver, or Appelles to paint with his pencil, as the comedy to life expresseth so many and various affections of the mind? There shall the spectator see some insulting with joy, others fretting with melancholy, raging with anger, mad with love, boiling with avarice, undone with riot, tortured with expectation, consumed with fear: no perturbation in common life but the orator finds an example of it in the scene. And then, for the elegancy of language, read but this inscription on the grave of a comic poet:[20]

Immortales mortales, si fas esset, flere,
Flerent divae Camoenae Naevium Poetam;
Itaque postquam est Orcino traditus thesauro,
Obliti sunt Romae, lingua loqui Latina;[21]

19 screen
20 Gnaeus Naevius, an early Roman writer of epic and drama
21 "If it were right to weep for mortals who have gained immortality, the goddess Muses would weep for Naevius. When he was given over to the treasure-house of Orcus, men at Rome forgot how to speak the Latin tongue."

or that modester testimony given by Lucius Aelius Stilo upon Plautus, who affirmed, *"Musas, si latine loqui voluissent, Plautino sermone fuisse loquuturas"*; [22] and that illustrious judgment by the most learned M. Varro[23] of him, who pronounced him the Prince of Letters and Elegancy in the Roman language.

I am not of that opinion to conclude a poet's liberty within the narrow limits of laws which either the grammarians or philosophers prescribe; for before they found out those laws there were many excellent poets that fulfilled them, amongst whom none more perfect than Sophocles, who lived a little before Aristotle. Which of the Greeklings durst ever give precepts to Demosthenes; or to Pericles, whom the age surnamed heavenly because he seemed to thunder and lighten with his language; or to Alcibiades, who had rather nature for his guide than art for his master?

But whatsoever nature at any time dictated to the most happy, or long exercise to the most laborious, that the wisdom and learning of Aristotle hath brought into an art, because he understood the causes of things, and what other men did by chance or custom he doth by reason, and not only found out the way not to err, but the short way we should take not to err.

Many things in Euripides hath Aristophanes wittily reprehended, not out of art, but out of truth; for Euripides is sometimes peccant,[24] as he is most times perfect. But judgment when it is greatest, if reason doth not accompany it, is not ever absolute. To judge of poets is only the faculty of poets, and not of all poets, but the best: *Nemo infaelicius de poetis judicavit, quam qui de poetis scripsit.*[25] But, some will say, critics are a kind of tinkers, that make more faults than they mend ordinarily: see their diseases, and those of the

22 "If the Muses had wanted to speak Latin, they would have used the language of Plautus."
23 Marcus Varro, called by Quintilian "the most learned of the Romans."
24 faulty
25 "No one has judged poets more falsely than he who scribbles about them."

grammarians. It is true many bodies are the worse for the meddling with, and the multitude of physicians hath destroyed many sound patients with their wrong practice; but the office of a true critic, or censor, is not to throw by a letter anywhere, or damn an innocent syllable, but lay the words together and amend them, judge sincerely of the author and his matter, which is the sign of solid and perfect learning in a man. Such was Horace, an author of much civility, and (if anyone among the heathen can be) the best master both of virtue and wisdom, an excellent and true judge upon cause and reason, not because he thought so, but because he knew so out of use and experience.

Cato, the grammarian, a defender of Lucilius . . . .[26]

Cato Grammaticus, Latina syren,
Qui solus legit et facit poetas.[27]

Quintilian of the same heresy, but rejected . . . .

Horace, his judgment of Chaerilus defended against Joseph Scaliger. And of Laberius against Julius . . . .

But chiefly his opinion of Plautus vindicated against many that are offended and say it is a hard censure upon the parent of all conceit and sharpness, and they wish it had not fallen from so great a master and censor in the art, whose bondmen knew better how to judge of Plautus than any that dare patronize the family of learning in this age; who could not be ignorant of the judgment of the times in which he lived, when poetry and the Latin language were at the height, especially being a man so conversant and inwardly familiar with the censures of great men that did discourse of these things daily amongst themselves; again a man so gracious, and in high favour with the Emperor, as Augustus often called him his witty *manling* (for the littleness of his stature), and, if we may trust antiquity, had designed him for a Secretary of State, and

[26] This, like the following sentences, is a suggestion for a further development of the treatise, or a note for the speaker to enlarge on.

[27] "Cato, the grammarian, the Latin Syren, who alone read and made poets": Suetonius.

invited him to the palace,[28] which he modestly prayed off and refused.

Horace did so highly esteem Terence his comedies as he ascribes the art in comedy to him alone among the Latins, and joins him with Menander.

Now let us see what may be said for either, to defend Horace his judgment to posterity, and not wholly to condemn Plautus . . . .[29]

The Parts of a Comedy and Tragedy

The parts of a comedy are the same with a tragedy, and the end is partly the same, for they both delight and teach: the comics are called *didaskaloi*[30] of the Greeks, no less than the tragics. Nor is the moving of laughter always the end of comedy, that is rather a fowling for the people's delight, or their fooling. For, as Aristotle says rightly, the moving of laughter is a fault in comedy, a kind of turpitude that depraves some part of a man's nature without a disease, as a wry face without pain moves laughter, or a deformed vizard, or a rude clown dressed in a lady's habit and using her actions: we dislike and scorn such representations, which made the ancient philosophers ever think laughter unfitting in a wise man. And this induced Plato to esteem of Homer as a sacrilegious person, because he presented the gods sometimes laughing: as also it is divinely said of Aristotle that to seem ridiculous is a part of dishonesty, and foolish.

So that, what either in the words or sense of an author, or in the language or actions of men, is awry or depraved doth strangely stir mean affections and provoke for the most part to laughter: and therefore it was clear that all insolent and obscene speeches, jest[s] upon the best men, injuries to particular persons, perverse and sinister sayings, and the rather unexpected, in the old comedy, did move to laughter, espe-

28 Folio: *place*
29 Something to follow this may have been projected and never written, or may have been lost; or the speaker may have continued lecturing extempore.
30 teachers

cially where it did imitate any dishonesty, and scurrility came forth in the place of wit; which who understands the nature and genius of laughter cannot but perfectly know. Of which Aristophanes affords an ample harvest, having not only outgone Plautus, or any other, in that kind, but expressed all the moods and figures of what is ridiculous oddly.

In short, as vinegar is not accounted good until the wine be corrupted, so jests that are true and natural seldom raise laughter with the beast, the multitude. They love nothing that is right and proper. The farther it runs from reason or possibility with them, the better it is. What could have made them laugh like to see Socrates presented, that example of all good life, honesty and virtue, to have him hoisted up with a pulley, and there play the philosopher in a basket, measure how many foot a flea could skip geometrically, by a just scale, and edify the people from the engine? [31] This was theatrical wit, right stage-jesting, and relishing a play-house invented for scorn and laughter; whereas if it had savoured of equity, truth, perspicuity, and candour, to have tasten a wise or a learned palate, spit it out presently – this is bitter and profitable: this instructs and would inform us: what need we know anything that are nobly born, more than a horse-race, or a hunting-match, our day to break with citizens, and such innate mysteries? This is truly leaping from the stage to the tumbril again, reducing all wit to the original dung-cart.

Of the magniture and compass of any fable, epic or dramatic: What the measure of a fable is

To the resolving of this opinion we must first agree in the definition of the fable. The fable is called the imitation of one entire and perfect action, whose parts are so joined and knit together as nothing in the structure can be changed or taken away without impairing or troubling the whole, of which there is a proportionable magnitude in the members. As, for example, if a man would build a house, he would first appoint a place to build it in, which he would define within certain

31 The reference is to Aristophanes' *Clouds*

bounds; so, in the constitution of a poem, the action is aimed at by the poet, which answers place in a building, and that action hath his largeness, compass, and proportion. So the epic asks a magnitude, from other poems: since, what is place in the one is action in the other, the difference is in space. So that by this definition we conclude the fable to be the *imitation* of one perfect and entire action, as one perfect and entire place is required to a building. By perfect, we understand that to which nothing is wanting, as place to the building that is raised, and action to the fable that is formed. It is perfect, perhaps, not for a court or king's palace, which requires a greater ground, but for the structure we would raise. So the space of the action may not prove large enough for the epic fable, yet be perfect for the dramatic, and whole.

What we understand by Whole

Whole, we call that, and perfect, which hath a *beginning*, a *midst*, and an *end*. So the place of any building may be whole and entire for that work, though too little for a palace. As to a tragedy or a comedy, the action may be convenient and perfect that would not fit an epic poem in magnitude. So a lion is a perfect creature in himself, though it be less than[32] a buffalo or a rhinoceros: they differ but in species: either in the kind is absolute. Both have their parts, and either the whole. Therefore, as in every body, so in every action which is the subject of a just work, there is required a certain proportionable greatness, neither too vast nor too minute: for that which happens to the eyes when we behold a body, the same happens to the memory when we contemplate an action. I look upon a monstrous giant, as Tityus,[33] whose body covered nine acres of land, and mine eye sticks upon every part: the whole that consists of those parts will never be taken in at one entire view. So in a fable, if the action be too great,

[32] Folio: *than that of a buffalo.* Castelain, following the orginal text of Heinsius, conjectures: *than an elephant. The head of a lion is a whole, though it be less than that of a buffalo*

[33] The giant whom Odysseus saw bound in Hades and covering nine roods of ground where he lay

we can never comprehend the whole together in our imagination. Again, if it be too little, there ariseth no pleasure out of the object: it affords the view no stay: it is beheld and vanisheth at once, as if we should look upon an ant or pismyre, the parts fly the sight and the whole considered is almost nothing. The same happens in action, which is the object of memory, as the body is of sight. Too vast oppresseth the eyes and exceeds the memory: too little scarce admits either.

What the utmost bounds of a fable

Now, in every action it behooves the poet to know which is his utmost bound, how far with fitness and a necessary proportion he may produce and determine it. That is, till either good fortune change into the worse, or the worse into the better. For, as a body without proportion cannot be goodly, no more can the action, either in comedy or tragedy, without his fit bounds; and every bound for the nature of the subject is esteemed the best that is the largest, till it can increase no more, so it behooves the action in tragedy or comedy to be let grow till the necessity ask a conclusion; wherein two things are to be considered: first, that it exceed not the compass of one day; next, that there be place left for digression and art. For the episodes and digressions in a fable are the same that household stuff and other furniture are in a house. And so far for the measure and extent of a fable dramatic.

What by one and entire

Now, that it should be one and entire. One is considerable two ways: either as it is only separate and by itself; or, as being composed of many parts, it begins to be one as those parts grow or are wrought together. That it should be one the first way alone, and by itself, no man that hath tasted letters ever would say, especially having required before a just magnitude and equal proportion of the parts in themselves, neither of which can possibly be, if the action be single and separate, not composed of parts which, laid together in themselves with an equal and fitting proportion, tend to the same end: which thing out of antiquity itself hath deceived many, and more this day it doth deceive.

So many there be of old that have thought the action of one man to be one: as of Hercules, Theseus, Achilles, Ulysses, and other heroes, which is both foolish and false, since by one and the same person many things may be severally done which cannot fitly be referred or joined to the same end – which not only the excellent tragic poets, but the best masters of the epic, Homer and Virgil, saw. For though the argument of an epic poem be far more diffused and poured out than that of tragedy, yet Virgil, writing of Aeneas, hath pretermitted[34] many things. He neither tells how he was born, how brought up, how he fought with Achilles, how he was snatched out of the battle by Venus, but that one thing, how he came into Italy, he prosecutes in twelve books. The rest of his journey, his error by sea, the sack of Troy, are put not as the argument of the work but episodes of the argument. So Homer laid by many things of Ulysses and handled no more than he saw tended to one and the same end.

Contrary to which, and foolishly, those poets did whom the philosopher taxeth: of whom, one gathered all the actions of Theseus, another put all the labours of Hercules in one work. So did he whom Juvenal mentions in the beginning, hoarse Codrus,[35] that recited a volume compiled, which he called his *Theseide,* not yet finished, to the great trouble both of his hearers and himself, amongst which there were many parts had no coherence nor kindred one with other, so far they were from being one action, one fable. For as a house consisting of diverse materials becomes one structure and one dwelling, so an action composed of diverse parts may become one fable, epic or dramatic. For example, in a tragedy, look upon Sophocles his Ajax: Ajax, deprived of Achilles' armour which he hoped from the suffrage of the Greeks, disdains, and, growing impatient of the injury, rageth and turns mad. In

34 omitted
35 Juvenal: *Satires* I, i. Codrus may have been a fictitious embodiment of the vain poetaster.

that humour he doth many senseless things, and at last falls upon the Grecian flock and kills a great ram for Ulysses. Returning to his sense, he grows ashamed of the scorn and kills himself, and is by the chiefs of the Greeks forbidden burial. These things agree and hang together, not as they were done, but as seeming to be done, which made the action whole, entire, and absolute.

The conclusion concerning the Whole and the Parts

For the whole, as it consisteth of parts, so, without all the parts, it is not the whole; and to make it absolute is required not only the parts but such parts as are true. For a part of the whole was true, which, if you take away, you either change the whole or it is not the whole. For if it be such a part as being present or absent nothing concerns the whole, it cannot be called a part of the whole: and such are the episodes, of which hereafter.[36] For the present, here is one example: the single combat of Ajax with Hector, as it is at large described in Homer, nothing belongs to this Ajax of Sophocles . . . .

36 This phrase shows the treatise, or series of lecture-notes, to be far from complete as we have it.

VI. OF LETTER-WRITING

In writing [letters] there is to be regarded the invention and the fashion. For the invention, that ariseth upon your business, whereof there can be no rules of more certainty, or precepts of better direction given than conjecture can lay down from the several occasions of men's particular lives and vocations. But sometimes men make business of kindness, as: "I could not satisfy myself till I had discharged my remembrance and charged my letter with commendations to you"; or, "My business is no other than to testify my love to you, and to put you in mind of my willingness to do you all kind offices"; or, "Sir, have you leisure to descend to the remembering of that assurance you have long possessed in your servant, and, upon your next opportunity, make him happy with some commands from you?" Or the like, that go a-begging for some meaning, and labour to be delivered of the great burden of nothing. When you have invented, and that your business be matter and not bare form or mere ceremony but some earnest, then are you to proceed to the ordering of it and digesting the parts, which is had out of two circumstances. One is the understanding of the persons to whom you are to write; the other is the coherence of your sentence. For men's capacity, to weigh what will be apprehended with greatest attention or leisure, what next regarded and longed for especially, and what last will leave satisfaction and, as it were, the sweetest memorial and brief of all that is past in his understanding whom you write to. For the consequence of sentences, you must be sure that every clause do give the cue one to the other and be bespoken ere it come. So much for the invention and order.

Now for the fashion, it consists in four things which are qualities of your style. The first is brevity: for they must not be treatises or discourses, your letters, except it be to learned men, and even among them there is a kind of thrift and saving of words. Therefore you are to examine the clearest passages of your understanding, and through them to convey the sweetest and most significant words you can devise; that you may the easier teach them the readiest way to another man's apprehension, and open their meaning fully, roundly, and distinctly: so as the reader may not think a second view cast away upon your letter. And though respect be a part following this, yet now, here, and still, I must remember it. If you write to a man whose estate and cense,[1] as senses[2] you are familiar with, you may the bolder, to set a task to his brain, venture on a knot. But if to your superior, you are bound to measure him in three farther points: first, your interest in him; secondly, his capacity in your letters; thirdly, his leisure to peruse them. For your interest or favour with him, you are to be the shorter or longer, more familiar or submiss, as he will afford you time. For his capacity, you are to be quicker and fuller of those reaches and glances of wit or learning as he is able to entertain them. For his leisure, you are commanded to the greater briefness as his place is of greater discharges and cares. But with your betters you are not to put riddles of wit by being too scarce of words, not to cause the trouble of making *breviates*[3] by writing too riotous and wastingly. Brevity is attained in matter by avoiding idle compliments, prefaces, protestations, parentheses, superfluous circuit of figures and digressions; in the composition by omitting conjunctions ("not only, but also"; "both the one and the other"; "whereby it cometh to pass") and such like idle particles that have no great business in a serious letter but breaking of sentences, as oftentimes a short journey is made long by unnecessary baits.

But, as Quintilian saith, there is a briefness of the parts sometimes that makes the whole long, as: "I came to the stairs, I took a pair of oars, they launched out, rowed a pace, I landed at the Court-gate, I paid my fare, went up to the presence, asked for my Lord, I was admitted." All this is but: "I went to the Court and spake with my Lord." This is the

1 social standing
2 matters (of perception)
3 summaries

fault of some Latin writers within these last hundred years, of my reading; and perhaps Seneca may be appeached of it: I accuse him not.

The next property of epistolary style is perspicuity, and is often-times, by[4] affectation of some wit, ill angled for, or ostentation of some hidden terms of art. Few words they darken speech: and so do too many: as well too much light hurteth the eyes as too little, and a long Bill of Chancery confounds the understanding as much as the shortest note. Therefore let not your letters be penned like English statutes and this is obtained. These vices are eschewed by pondering your business well and distinctly conceiving yourself, which is much furthered by uttering your thoughts and letting them as well come forth to the light and judgment of your own outward senses as to the censure of other men's ears: for that is the reason why many good scholars speak but fumblingly, like a rich man that, for want of particular note and difference, can bring you no certain ware readily out of his shop. Hence it is that talkative shallow men do often content the hearers more than the wise. But this may find a speedier redress in writing, where all comes under the last examination of the eyes. First mind it well, then pen it, then examine it, then amend it, and you may be in the better hope of doing reasonably well.

Under this virtue may come plainness, which is not to be curious in the order, as to answer a letter as if you were to answer to interrogatories (as to the first, first; and to the second, secondly, etc.), but both in method [and words][5] to use, as ladies do in their attire, a diligent kind of negligence and their sportive freedom. Though with some men you are not to jest or practise tricks, yet the delivery of the most important things may be carried with such a grace as that it may yield a pleasure to the conceit of the reader. There must be store though no excess of terms: as, if you are to name

4 Herford and Simpson, restoring from the passage in *Directions for Speech*, by John Hoskyns, which Jonson is here transcribing: *often-times indangered by the former qualitie (brevity), often-times by affectation*
5 Herford and Simpson conj. (after Hoskyns)

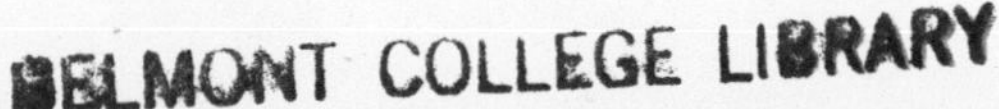

store, sometimes you may call it *choice,* sometimes *plenty,* sometimes *copiousness* or *variety,* but ever so that the word which comes in lieu have not such difference of meaning as that it may put the sense of the first in hazard to be mistaken. You are not to cast a ring for the perfumed terms of the time, as *accommodation, compliment, spirit,* etc., but use them properly in their place, as others.

There followeth life and quickness, which is the strength and sinews, as it were, of your penning, by pretty sayings, similitudes and conceits, allusions [to] some known history or other commonplace, such as are in the *Courtier*[6] and the second book of *Cicero de Oratore.*

The last is respect to discern what fits yourself, him to whom you write, and that which you handle; which is a quality fit to conclude the rest, because it doth include all: and that must proceed from ripeness of judgment, which, as one truly saith, is gotten by four means — God, nature, diligence, and conversation. Serve the first well and the rest will serve you.

6 Castiglione's *Il Cortegiano,* best known in the English translation by Sir Thomas Hoby as *The Courtier.*

VII. RANDOM NOTES

(Scraps suggesting character or dialogue suitable for comedy)

He hath a delicate wife, a fair fortune and family to go to [to] be welcome; yet he had rather be drunk with mine host and the fiddlers of such a town than go home.

Affliction teacheth a wicked person sometime to pray; prosperity never.

Many might go to heaven with half the labour they go to hell, if they would venture their industry the right way; but, "The devil take all," quoth he that was choked i' the mill-dam with his four last words in his mouth.

A cripple in the way out-travels a footman or a post out of the way.

Bags of money to a prodigal person are the same that cherry-stones are with some boys, and so thrown away.

A woman, the more curious she is about her face, is commonly the more careless about her house.

Of this spilt water there is little to be gathered up: it is a desperate debt.

The thief with a great belly that had a longing at the gallows to commit one robbery more before he was hanged; and like the German lord,[1] [who] when he went out of Newgate into the cart, took order to have his arms set up in his last herborough,[2] said he was taken and committed upon suspicion of treason, no witness appearing against him. But the judges entertained him most civilly, discoursed with him, offered him the courtesy of the rack, but he confessed, etc.

I am beholden to calumny, that she hath so endeavoured and taken pains to belie me. It shall make me set a surer guard on myself and keep a better watch upon my actions.

A tedious person is one a man would leap a steeple from; gallop down any steep hill to avoid him; forsake his meat, sleep, nature itself with all her benefits, to shun him; a mere

1 Folio: (marginal note) *Com. de Schortenhien*
2 lodging-place

impertinent, one that touched neither heaven nor earth in his discourse. He opened an entry into a fair room, but shut it again presently. I spake to him of garlic, he answered asparagus; consulted him of marriage, he tells me of hanging, as if they went by one and the same destiny.

That an elephant, 630, came hither ambassador from the great Mogul, who could both write and read, and was every day allowed twelve cast of bread, twenty quarts of canary sack, besides nuts and almonds the citizens' wives sent him. That he had a Spanish boy to his interpreter, and his chief negotiation was to confer or practise with Archie, the principal fool of state, about stealing hence Windsor Castle[3] and carrying it away on his back if he can.

Do but ask of nature why all living creatures are less delighted with meat and drink, that sustains them, than with venery, that wastes them; and she will tell thee, the first respects but a private, the other, a common good, propagation.

You admire no poems but such as run like a brewer's cart upon the stones, hobbling,

Et quae per salebras altaque saxa cadunt.[4]
Accius[5] *et quidquid Pacuviusque vomunt.*[6]
Attonitusque legis terrai frugiferai.[7]

[3] The crest of the Cutlers' Company consisted of an elephant bearing a castle on its back.

[4] "Which pass over rough roads and huge rocks."

[5] Folio: *Actius*

[6] "Whatever Accius and Pacuvius have disgorged."

[7] "Astonished you read 'terrai frugiferai'." These three lines are all from Martial's Epigram *To Chrestillus, an absurd admirer of the poets of antiquity* (XI, xc), which must have been a favourite of Jonson's since he quotes it three times in the *Discoveries.* The gist of the Epigram is as follows: "You approve of no verses that run smoothly, but of those only which bump along over rough roads and great rocks; and a line such as this *'Luceilei columella heic situ' Metrophan' est'* (Lucilius's right-hand, Metrophanes, lies here) is of more worth in your eyes than a poem by Homer. You read with ecstacy such words as *'terrai frugiferai'* (the fruit-bearing earth) and all that Accius and Pacuvius have belched forth. Do you want me to imitate these old poets, Chrestillus, whom you admire so much? I'm damned if I think you know what vigorous writing is!"

A LIST OF THE PRINCIPAL SOURCES

Showing alterations to the order in the 1640-41 folio made in this edition.

Line-references are to Herford and Simpson's edition, Vol. VIII (1947).

Passages borrowed or translated by Jonson are given in their original form in the notes to Herford and Simpson's edition, Vol. XI (1952).

I. Essays:

1. Of Flatterers *(lines 1586-1635)*
2. Of the Diversity of Wits *(669-800, 846-861, 948-958)*
   Quintilian, *De Institutione Oratoria;* Seneca, *Epistolae ad Lucilium;* M. Seneca, *Controversiae.*
3. Of Envy (258-321)
   Scaliger, *Confutatio Stultissimae Burdonum Fabulae*
4. Of Talking Overmuch (330-404)
   Aulus Gellius, *Noctes Atticae;* Plutarch, *De Garrulitate;* Erasmus, *Lingua;* Plautus, *Trinummus;* Mignault, *Omnia Andreae Alciati V.C. Emblemata*
5. Of Worthless Aims (1323-1467)
   Apuleius, *De Magia;* Seneca, *Epist.*
6. Of Picture and Poetry (1509-1540, 1549-1585)
   Quintilian, *Inst. Orat.;* Possevino, *Bibliotheca Selecta Qua Agitur De Ratione Studiorum*

II. Of Learning to Read Well, Speak Well and Write Well

1. Introductory Letter (1636-1696, 1787-1820)
   Quintilian, *Inst. Orat.*
2. Of Diligence in Learning (1821-1862, 821-845, 218-226, 1863-1868, 1873-1880, 1868-1873, 862-883)
   Quintilian, *Inst. Orat.* M. Seneca, *Controv.*
3. Of Language in Oratory (1881-2089, 1541-1548, 116-123) Quintilian, *Inst. Orat.;* Vives, *De Ratione Dicendi; In Libros de Disciplinis Praefatio*
4. Of Judging Poets and Poetry (2290-2345, 1020-1045, 587-668, 570-586)

Erasmus, *Epistola Apologetica ad Martinum Dorpium Theologium;* M. Seneca, *Controv.;* Quintilian, *Inst. Orat.*

5. Of Liberal Studies (160-174, 924-947, 2090-2124, 129-159)

   Vives, *De Causis Corruptarum Artium; In Libros De Disciplinis;* M. Seneca, *Controv.*

6. Of Writing Well (2125-2160, 1697-1754, 884-923, 228-235, 124-128, 1755-1787)

   Hoskyns, *Directions for Speech and Style;* Quintilian, *Inst. Orat.;* M. Seneca, *Controv.;* Vives, *In Libros De Disciplinis.*

III. Explorata, or Discoveries (1-59, 175-178, 236-241, 251-257, 404-569, 801-820, 959-966, 1046-1115, 1298-1305, 1468-1508, 60-64)

"Fortuna": Seneca, *Consolatio ad Helviam.*
"Amor Patriae": Euripides, *Phoenissae.*
"Ingenia": Quintilian, *Inst. Orat.*
"Applausus": Velleius Paterculus, *Ex Historiae Romanae*
"Jactura Vita": Quintilian, *Inst. Orat.*
"Honesta Ambitio": Pliny, *Epist.*
"Impostorum Fucus": Bacon, *De Augmentis Scientiarum*
"Vulgi Expectatio": M. Seneca, *Controv.*
"Eloquentia": M. Seneca, *Controv.*
"Amor et Odium": Seneca, *De Beneficiis*
"Injuriae": Seneca, *De Beneficiis*
"Beneficia": Seneca, *De Beneficiis*
"Valor Rerum": Seneca, *De Beneficiis*
"Memoria": M. Seneca, *Controv.*
"Comit. Suffragia": Pliny, *Epist.*
"Deus in Creaturis": Justus Lipsius, *Politica*
"Veritas Proprium Hominis": Justus Lipsius, *Politica*
"Nullum Vitium sine Patrocinio": Seneca, *Epist.*
"De Rebus Mundanis": Seneca, *Epist.*

"Controvers, Scriptores": Erasmus, *Hyperaspites Diatribae*

"Jactantia Intempestiva": Pliny, *Epist.*

"Adulatio": Seneca, *Quaestiones Naturales*

"Periculosa Melancholia": Seneca, *Epist.*

"Falsae Species Fugiendae": Plutarch, *Moralia*

IV. Of Statecraft (1003-1019, 1234-1249, 242-250, 1291-1297, 65-115, 1127-1138, 1306-1322, 972-991, 1139-1177, 992-1002, 1178-1212, 1116-1126, 1213-1233, 1250-1291)

Erasmus, *Institutio Oratoria;* Franciscus Patricius, *De Regno et Regis Institutione;* Justus Lipsius, *Politica;* H. Farnese, *Diphthera Iouis;* Plutarch, *De Adulatore et Amico;* Machiavelli, *Il Principe;* Seneca, *De Clementia;* Suetonius, *Caligula;* Vives, *Epistola Nuncupatoria; De Consultatione.*

V. The Art of Poetry (2346-2815)

Aristotle, *Poetics;* J. Buchler, *Institutio Poetica;* Scaliger, *Poetices Libri Septem;* Cicero, *Pro Archia Poeta; De Oratore;* Seneca, *Epist.; De Tranquillitate Animi;* Valerius Maximus, *De Dictis et Factis Memorabilis;* Daniel Heinsius, *De Tragoediae Constitutione; Ad Horatium de Plauto et Terentio Judicium Dissertatio;* Quintilian, *Inst. Orat.*

VI. Of Letter Writing (2161-2289)

Hoskyns, *Directions for Speech and Style.*

VII. Random Notes (179-218, 322-329, 967-971, 2816-2820)

BEN JONSON'S LYRIC POETRY

Ben Jonson's non-dramatic poems are usually classified, for convenience of discussion rather than because the division suggests any clear-cut distinction, into two main groups: in the one, the Epigrams (using the term in the very broad sense which both Martial and Jonson give it, to include epistles, satires and various kinds of occasional poem) and in the other, the Lyrics, under which head are included the songs, odes, and hymns. Except for the well-known epitaphs, those of the first group made no strong appeal to nineteenth-century tastes, and their considerable poetical merits have not, as far as I know, had much recognition in recent times. The best of those in the second group have never lacked praise, though I think they have often been praised for the wrong reasons.

His poetry may also be divided in a way which does not coincide with this formal classification, and which is more critically suggestive, into three types of verse: a lyrical verse inspired by a classical ideal of art; a lyrical verse inspired by a romantic ideal; and a verse which, whether it be dramatic, epigrammatic, satirical, narratival, or descriptive, has, as a primary consideration, "body" or good sense, and makes a direct appeal to the intellect, as well as to the emotions and the imagination. The first and third are closely related, as products of the same system of thought and feeling, but it is unusual for one man to excel in the first and second kinds, whose aims and methods are so different that different standards of judgment are called for in assessing them: yet Jonson is both the supreme exponent in English of the classical lyric, and at times an effective practitioner of the romantic.

The seventeenth century was not obtuse to the nature of Jonson's achievement in the lyric. There is no disputing its historical importance in the evolution of seventeenth-century poetical styles, for Jonson's influence can be shown to be at least equal to that of Donne in furthering the reaction against the Spenserian tradition; but the lavish encomiums of Jonson's contemporaries and immediate successors, since they are themselves in lyrical form, are of only partial validity as criticism.[1] Shirley, Herrick, Marmion, and a host of minor poets paid tribute to Jonson, as to their spiritual father, but it is in their practice as lyric-writers that they reveal the nature of their debt to him, not in their direct references to his poetry. The eighteenth century had its attention directed by Dryden to the drama, as being the most significant field of Jonson's experiments,[2] and it is doubtful if the Augustans, with their Frenchified classicism, though certainly much influenced in styles and techniques by the writings of the school of Jonson, ever realized what it was that Jonson, through his much clearer conception of the underlying ideal of classical art, achieved in the best of his lyrics. Nineteenth-century critics saw Ben Jonson primarily as a wrong-headed dramatist whose plays contrasted unfavourably with Shakespeare's: they felt the appeal of his characteristic lyrics, but because these did not conform with their preconceptions of the nature of lyric poetry, they were at a loss to explain it, and wrote of them with a curious ambiguity, hesitation, or even annoyance. Thus Symonds, after much searching for the qualities which are least distinctive in it, dismisses Jonson's lyrical verse with: "For Jonson's fame it is quite enough to point out that these, rather than Shakespeare's lyrics, struck the keynote of the seventeenth century";[3] Gregory Smith "hesitates when he

1 As e.g. in *Jonsonus Virbius*, 1638; Herrick's Epigrams *Upon M. Ben Jonson*, in *Hesperides*, 1648; and the commendatory verses prefixed to the various seventeenth-century editions of Jonson's *Works*.

2 Dryden's *Essay of Dramatick Poesie*, 1668; *A Defence of an Essay of Dramatick Poesie*, 1668; and the Preface to *An Evening's Love; or the Mock Astrologer*, 1671

3 *Ben Jonson*, by John Addington Symonds, 1886

comes to consider Jonson as a poet," and expresses, "with a farmerly touch of annoyance," his surprise at the indefinability of his lyric success;[4] Saintsbury is no less troubled by "the anomalous and seemingly contradictory power" of his lyrical "grace and sweetness";[5] and Swinburne pauses, in the course of a lengthy paean of praise for his lyric verse, to indicate "its crowning and damning defect." [6]

I suggest that the reason these Victorian critics were at a loss to understand the nature of Ben Jonson's achievement was because they were accustomed to evaluating lyric poetry according to the apparent spontaneity of the emotion expressed in it. Where his lyrics can be appreciated for romantic qualities, possess incantatory power or release a ready flow of feeling, they commend them; but when faced by a verse which is clearly the product of a conscious art, which never denies its consciousness but is nevertheless beautiful and moving, they are obliged either to ignore it in their criticism or involve themselves in contradictions. The lyric was then widely believed to be, as Pater says, "the highest and most complete form of poetry" and the romantics held it as their especial province: baffled by Jonson's most characteristic experiments in that form, they passed over his lyric verse and regarded him chiefly as a dramatist, easily vulnerable by their favourite test of drama (the profundity and subtlety of its characterisation) and readily explained away by the dwarfing process of comparison with Shakespeare.

As a dramatist, he has received a measure of understanding appreciation in our own time, and we have come to realize that a comparison between Shakespeare and Jonson is misleading unless it is used to emphasise their essential difference of intention, and the consequent incommensurability of their achievement. But even when it is recognised that the beauty and emotional impulse of *Volpone* and *Catiline* are revealed

[4] *Ben Jonson,* by G. Gregory Smith, 1926
[5] *Elizabethan Literature,* by George Saintsbury, 1887
[6] *A Study of Ben Jonson,* by Algernon Charles Swinburne, 1889

less in detail than in the structure of the play as a finished entity (a significant point in the understanding of Jonson's art in all its branches), it remains true that his most original, most impeccable, and most influential successes were not the plays, but the best of the lyric poems.

His plays are all experimental, and each has its significance as a manifestation of the general conception of beauty and of art which underlay his practice; but they do not, in any single case afford more than a partial outlet for its expression. In no single play are the peculiar elements which go to the making of Jonson's individual sensibility synthesized and brought to perfect fruition. They are dispersed among the plays: in the lyrics alone they blend at times into a harmony which permits of full and satisfactory self-expression. And I believe that it was because no Victorian critic recognized in Jonson's "classical" lyrics a form of self-expression of a profound and fundamental kind, that they appeared so unaccountable in their perfection, gave rise to so much hedging on the part of commentators, and seem to have proved a source of uneasiness and mystification rather than pleasure.

If his dramatic poems are experimental, most of his other poems, in their conscious striving after form, are of that nature, too. Even in his lyric style however, there is no normal evolutionary growth from one phase to another of lessening imperfection: success is occasional and spasmodic. His whole artistic development, with its extraordinary variety and exuberance, appears to be without systematic progression, partly because it is not the result of a mere subconscious urge, but is directed by theory in all sorts of different directions in the process of trial and error. His poetic sensibility, seeking adequate expression, is forever pushing towards the surface in one direction and then, meeting some repulse, in another; for the poet's critical mind, striving to mold the literary conventions of his day to suit his highly original ends, is hard put to it to contrive poetical forms adapted to his individual and revolutionary genius. There are not many among his lyrics which can be called perfect in all respects, though there are many which show in some degree those qualities of shapeliness, finish, and impersonality which belong to the supreme successes. Many of the songs in the masques have a formal beauty which they owe largely to the fact that they were written as a basis for musical composition and in careful conformity with the technique of Elizabethan part-singing:[7] some of these masque-songs are artificial, gimcrack affairs, but the discipline involved in shaping them to a pattern was plainly of value in helping Jonson to evolve a lyric style which could express the essence of his classicism. Where his conception of the beautiful finds expression in a form which perfectly agrees with his ideal of art we have a poetry with a pure, cold, unromantic loveliness, as in the three songs *To Celia,*[8] the *Hymn to Diana,*[9] *Her Triumph* (from the *Celebration of Charis*),[10] *O do not Wanton with those Eyes,*[11] *Still to be Neat,*[12] *Follow a Shadow,*[13] and *Slow, Slow fresh Fount.*[14]

Contrast the poetry of romance with the poetry of such lyrics and it is apparent that the aesthetic perception actuating the two is fundamentally different. From the velvety woodbines and sleek marigolds of Keats, to turn to this:

> So love emergent out of chaos brought
>   The world to light,
> And gently moving on the waters wrought
>   All forms to sight[15]

is like turning from some warm, lush meadow of actual experience, to a cool, paved terrace, erected, not in the outer world, but in the stillness of the mind. Jonson's conception of beauty does not to the same extent involve appreciation of external

7 See *Ben Jonson and Elizabethan Music,* by W. M. Evans, 1929
8 *The Forrest,* V, VI, and IX
9 *Cynthia's Revels,* V, iii
10 *The Underwood,* II, iv
11 *The Underwood,* IV
12 *Epicoene, or the Silent Women,* I, i
13 *The Forrest,* VII
14 *Cynthia's Revels,* I, i
15 Hymn of Euclia, in *Love's Triumph through Callipolis*

phenomena: his themes are not evoked through an emotional sympathy with the autumn sky or the nightingale's song. Instead of springing from the contemplation of variety and diversity in man and nature, his beauty belongs to the apprehension of their underlying symmetry. It is the harmony and finish of the scheme of things which is beautiful to him, and not any incidental development in nature. His idea of beauty is intimately connected with the balance of the universe, the order and rhythm of the spheres, the perfection of adjustment underlying the irregularity of outward forms.

But the inspiration of Jonson's poetry, as manifested in these "classical" lyrics, is not the abstract idea of this symmetry, so much as the idea realized in the ordered working of a finished creation. It is as if the poet saw the world as an architect might see a cathedral, impressed not so much by its surface beauty and ornamentation, nor yet concerned with its original conception as an idea, or a plan on paper, but moved to exultation at the mathematical precision of design revealed in the perfect structure. The mystic sees in every form of outward manifestation only an imperfect shadow of the idea behind it, and rejoices in a perfection which is half-concealed, half-formulated. But for Jonson it is "love emergent out of chaos" which brings the world to light: the unfulfilled idea with all its possibilities is not what moves him, for it remains imperfect until it had found expression. Jonson's highest beauty is a beauty of completion: "it might be" is beautiful only when it has become "it is." And because his ideal beauty is thus intimately linked with the creative act, where it finds adequate expression it does so in a finished and conscious art.

All the characteristic qualities of Jonson's classical lyrics at their best demonstrate, in their own particulars, the essential components of his ideal of beauty:

> It was a beauty that I saw,
> So pure, so perfect.[16]

16 *The New Inn*, IV, iii

The all-pervading restraint of *An Hymn to Diana,*[17] the simple economy of utterance in the verses *To the Author of 'The Touchstone of Truth,'* [18] the even movement, directness of language and naked dignity of style towards which he strives and which, at times, he achieves, together with the ordered management and finished execution which give his stanzas their effect of balanced finality: all these are expressions of those central principles of purity and perfection which comprise Ben Jonson's idea of beauty.

If such a conception of beauty is essentially that of the "classical" as opposed to the romantic in poetry, it seems to me that nowhere in English poetry has it found such complete expression as in a few of Jonson's lyrics. It recurs in the poetry of his seventeenth century successors, but in a modified and derivative form. Pope and the Augustans were pseudo-classicists of a modernized type; and Professor Herford was surely mistaken when he called Jonson "a precursor of the Augustans, imperfectly grasping the ideals they were destined to achieve." [19] The Tudor and Elizabethan writers of the English renaissance, again, were Italianate and essentially romantic, despite their superficial devotion to certain classical principles. Only in Ben Jonson is there complete absorption of the abstract and barely definable spirit usually indicated by the epithet "classical."

Because he did arrive at his conception of ideal truth and beauty by a process of absorption and selection, through constant study of the poets and critics of antiquity, there has been a tendency in the past to deny his originality. Some of his most successful lyrics are directly inspired by Horace and Catullus: "you may track him everywhere in their snow," [20] as Dryden said. But except by means of imitation and absorption

[17] *Cynthia's Revels,* V, iii

[18] Complimentary verses prefixed to *The Triumph of Truth, by* T. Warre, 1630

[19] *Life of Ben Jonson,* in *Ben Jonson,* edited by C. H. Herford and Percy Simpson, vol. I, 1925.

[20] *Essay of Dramatick Poesie,* 1668

there can be no originality: the greatest originators have the longest tradition behind their art. It is only by a reverent absorption of the spirit and wisdom of the past that originality is achieved, and the more complete the absorption the more fundamental the originality is likely to be. The unoriginal poet accepts without absorption and his expression lacks individuality because his inspiration is of shallow root and imperfectly realized. Jonson, steeped in the spirit of a refined and purified classicism, was faced with the necessity of developing a new and individual mode of expression: to it he owed that original perspicacity which made him more clearly aware than his contemporaries of the tawdriness and insincerity of the overhandled Elizabethan style. He set himself to evolve a new and original style, but he did so because he had something new to express, an ideal of beauty never before expressed in English poetry.

Those who deny originality to Ben Jonson are generally those who most admire his less original work. Had he lingered only where

> In the stocks of trees white faies do dwell,
> And spanlong elves that dance about a pool
> With each a little changeling in their arms;[21]

had he relied for inspiration on his invocation to Fancy:

> Break, Phant'sie, from thy cave of cloud,
> And spread thy purple wings;
> Now all thy figures are allowed,
> And various shapes of things;
> Create of airy forms a stream . . . .
> And though it be a waking dream,
> Yet let it like an odour rise
> To all the senses here,
> And fall like sleep upon their eyes,
> Or music in their ear,[22]

he would have attained a certain minor success in the Eliza-

21 *The Sad Shepherd*, II, ii
22 *The Vision of Delight*

bethan tradition. But he seldom rises to any considerable height on these borrowed "purple wings." And it is the constant lament of his nineteenth century critics that he did not assume them oftener. "That singing power," says Swinburne, "hardly now and then could his industry attain to it by some exceptional touch of inspiration or of luck." Gregory Smith finds him "rarely, if indeed ever, possessed by compelling song. He has no passion." There is more penetration in Symond's verdict: "If the haunting evanescent exquisiteness of Shakespeare's song is absent, we have not the right to demand this from a singer of so different a mould." His romantic poems are, as a rule, unsatisfactory, because of the sense of insecurity, the half-insincerity, which pervades them and gives them what Coleridge might have called their "inconstancy." When he weaves a gauzy fabric of romance with borrowed silks, he is apt to tear it suddenly and brutally, as if impatient at his own pretence. It is a practice similar to, yet not so effective as, the habit in his drama of checking and "debunking" a flight of Marlowesque extravagance by harsh or cynical comment; as Sir Epicure Mammon's rhapsody is checked and deflated by Surly's muttered asides.[23] The unexpected relapse into an incongruous, contrasting key, for which Scott dubbed him "coarse," [24] is typical of his experiments in the purely Elizabethan, is parallelled by his inclusion of the Maudlin-Lorel dialogue in the *Sad Shepherd*,[25] and indicates the unsuitability of the medium to his needs as a lyrical poet. It can be illustrated in the song just quoted from the *Vision of Delight*, whose sixth line, omitted above, runs:

It must have blood and nought of phlegm

That Ben Jonson frequently returned to essay the Elizabethan mode was partly due, perhaps, to the desire for appreciation which is never wholly absent from the creative mind, however stern its dedication to a higher end. And to write an Elizabethan pastoral was to make a stronger bid for popular

23 *The Alchemist*, II, i
24 *Life of Dryden*, by Sir Walter Scott, 1808.
25 *The Sad Shepherd*, II, ii

applause and understanding than to write *Sejanus*. Nor are the opening lines of the *Sad Shepherd* without their own beauty:

> Here she was wont to go! and here! and here!
> Just where those daisies, pinks and violets grow:
> The world may find the spring by following her,
> For other print her airy steps ne'er left.

But they represent a mere reorganization of exhausted elements according to a recognized formula. The freshness is due to a momentary recapturing of the *Midsummer Night's Dream* atmosphere, a fleeting glimpse which is gone as quickly as it came. And the masques, though they possess their own peculiar merits, contain little poetry apart from the occasional isolated lyrics which stand out from their framework like precious stones in a setting of tinsel.

In the pre-eminently successful lyrics, like the *Song of Celia*[26] and the *Hymn to Diana*,[27] emotional impulse and craftsmanship are inextricably combined. The beauty expressed in the finished lyric is a beauty which belongs to, and cannot be expressed otherwise than in craftsmanship. The conscious artistry of Ben Jonson's lyric style is a cause and a result of his poetic emotion: and so his rarest singing lyrics make no attempt to disown their conscious engineering of design. The complicated internal balance of the *Triumph of Charis*,[28] the careful and almost monosyllabic simplicity of *An Hymn to God the Father:*

> If Thou hadst not
> Been stern to me,
> I had forgot
> Myself and Thee . . .[29]

are essential products of that restraint and finish which belong to Ben Jonson's art. If his lyrics have a frigid and translucent beauty like that of a crystal cameo, they are like a cameo also

26 *The Forest*, No. IX
27 *Cynthia's Revels*, V, iii
28 *The Underwood*, II, iv
29 *The Underwood*, I, ii

in their unashamed avowal of the carver's hand. The form of the finished lyric is itself an emotional product, for form and system are intrinsic factors in Jonson's ideal of beauty. His lyric at its best possesses a peculiar integrity of its own: it seems to express nothing beyond or behind itself, but, in its final state, to be itself the idea which it expresses.

It is this fact which must baulk romantic criticism in any effort to appreciate Ben Jonson. It can appreciate the frame of mind which gave birth to a penitential poem like *An Hymn to God the Father,* or the pathos of the *Epitaph on Salathiel Pavy;*[30] it can acclaim the occasional liberation of emotion from its framework which occurs in lines like these:

> O had I now your manner, mastery, might,
> Your power of handling shadow, air and spright,
> How I would draw, and take hold and delight! [31]

But it cannot take the hint contained in the substance of these lines: it cannot account for lyrics like the *Vision of Beauty*[32] or the *Birth of Love.*[33] For expression, to a romantic poet like Shelley, is always imperfect, always embodying something which it is inadequate to contain. And to a critic possessed of such a theory as to the function of form in poetry, it is only natural to suspect in Jonson's best work an element of insincerity. But there is a difference between attempting to express a preconceived state of consciousness and evolving an emotional state by expressing it. Different standards have to be applied to poetry which is a means, like that of Shelley, and poetry which is an end, like Ben Jonson's. In its very skilfulness Jonson's poetry is eminently sincere, and its craft-consciousness is not something over which Symonds, Swinburne, and Gregory Smith need be disparaging or even apologetic.

The formal nature of Jonson's subconscious ideal of beauty belongs equally to his conscious ideal for art, an ideal which becomes apparent in his critical utterances. It has been said

[30] *Epigrams* CXX
[31] *The Poet to the Painter,* in *Underwoods*
[32] *The New Inn,* IV, iii
[33] *The Masque of Beauty*

that he made no original contribution to Renaissance criticism, that he merely restated a position fully formulated in the writings of critics like Sidney, Webbe, and Puttenham. They, too, had been concerned about the prevalence of poetastry, and had seen salvation for the "rakehelly rout of ragged rhymesters" and "pottical, poetical heads" in a redisciplining of art on classical lines. Moreover Jonson's *Discoveries,* like his lyrics, consist largely of free translations from Greek and Latin. But his originality in criticism, as in poetry, is an originality of absorption and comprehension which finds an outlet in practice as well as in theory. More than any of his predecessors, he bound himself over to the accomplishment of his artistic ideal, and to its furthering in English literature.

The state of poetry which roused such a vigorous reforming zeal in Jonson was a decadent one; that is to say its conventions had become outworn, and were no longer applicable to the changed attitude of men towards their changed conditions. As Young Lorenzo puts it, in *Every Man in His Humour,* poetry seemed now

> Patched up in remnants and old worn rags,
> Half starved for want of her peculiar food.[34]

The bastard classical tradition, which English literature inherited from Renaissance Italy, had provided an ideal outlet for the exuberant vitality of an awakening world. The youthful overflow of Elizabethan spirits had found artistic expression in extreme naiveté, and in extreme artificiality; for the simplicity and affectation of Elizabethan poetry are both, in their opposite ways, effects of that comparative immaturity of mind which marks the age. But the clear-eyed simplicity of a lyric by Peele was too genuine a thing to outlast its incentive: its freshness belonged to the dawn and could not survive it. The Golden Pomp, abandoning simplicity, sought to express itself in rhetoric and rhodomontade. But with the decline of that spirit of optimism which could put genuineness into the rant of a Marlowe, the sustaining fabric of sincerity dwindled

[34] *Every Man in his Humour,* V, i

and the empty shell of affectation remained. Artfulness in phraseology, from being a tenderly nourished acquisition, became almost an unnatural passion:

> Taffeta phrases, silken terms precise,
> Three-piled hyperboles, spruce affectation,
> Figures pedantical; these summer flies[35]

blew the style of Lyly's euphuistic imitators "full of maggot ostentation." The pursuit of literature degenerated into a scramble after "archaic, inkhorn, oversea" phraseology. Bacon could diagnose "the distemper of learning" as consisting in "the whole inclination of the times rather towards copy than weight," [36] Shakespeare could parody the mannerisms of the day in the absurd effusion of Holofernes, and Jonson was moved to indignation at the "greedy fry" too easily

> taken with false baits
> Of worded balladry.[37]

The deepening cast of thought which characterises the Jacobean period rendered it impossible for poetry to seek salvation in any effort to exchange its artificiality for the graceful carelessness of the early Elizabethan style. Past methods were too flimsy to express the new complexities of a maturer age. Thought tended to become increasingly subjective, and elation of the senses was no longer a sufficient impetus to verse-writing. The lyric, to survive, must prepare to convey more strenuous experiences than it had previously done, must adapt itself to bear a new intensity of meaning, and to express a more personal and reflective mood. Jonson's lyric style at its height does not fulfil these temporal demands upon the genre, although it furthers their fulfilment. It is peculiar in its lack of any profound or even apparent moral value, since it is not, to a normal degree, inspired by a personal experience previous to its embodiment in a poem, but seems to spring somehow out of the experience of creation. But Jonson was well

[35] *Love's Labours Lost,* V, iii
[36] *Advancement of Learning,* Book I
[37] *An Ode.—To Himself; The Underwood,* XXIII

aware of the tendency of the times towards increased profundity of thought, and of the incapacity of existing poetic conventions to cope with habits of critical self-searching. The style of his occasional verse, compliment, epitaph and epigram, is an effect of this awareness. And as a critic he saw in himself a Horace, and in his contemporaries the infatuated sons of Pompilius: "What is so furious and Bedlam-like as a vain sound of chosen and excellent words without any subject of sentence and science mixed?" [38]

More alive than Webbe to "the cankered enmity of curious custom," more aware than Harvey of what constitutes a "right artificiality," Jonson applies to the prevalent disease a panacea compounded of simplicity and restraint, craftsmanship, sincerity, and wit. His real and infinite debt to the classics is not to be gauged by uncovering the sources of his adaptations. It is to be found in his recognition, brought about by his acquaintance with the classics, that true wit does not consist in mere word-play, and that decadent Elizabethan verse-craftsmanship was a craftsmanship wrongly applied and of a self-destructive nature. By his frankness, his directness of style and his glorification of "good sense," he seeks to confound the mishandlers of the Petrarchian involution and exalt that "language such as men do use" which is commended in the prologue to *Every Man in his Humour.* And he supports his practice by many a frontal assault on meaningless verbal sensationalism: it is for trafficking in such verbiage that Crispinus is punished in the *Poetaster.*[39]

The reaction against the Spenserian tradition in lyric poetry was not due in its inception solely to Jonson. Reaction against excess in any one direction may take the form of a reversion to normality; more often it develops into a violent swing in an opposite direction. Both these tendencies are visible in Jacobean poetry, and it is perhaps because Donne's influence was, in a sense, eccentric, that it was more immediate but less en-

38 *Timber, or Discoveries*
39 *Poetaster,* V. i

during than Jonson's. Jonson's influence is formal in the widest sense. It takes account of the needs of poetry as an evolutionary force. It is not primarily concerned with the temporary situation, but reaches out to what is permanent in art. To Donne poetic form is something of an encumbrance, an intractable medium which must be controlled lest it control. For before Donne seized it and wrested it victoriously to his needs, the lyric had not passed through any phase of preparation for his coming. The very suddenness of the change it had to undergo in his hands lessened the enduring effect of his influence. Jonson, although he "esteemeth John Donne the first poet in the world, in some things," believed "that Donne himself, for not being understood, would perish." [40] And it is true that, in comparison with an impersonal poet like the Ben Jonson of

Queen and huntress, chaste and fair,

Donne's appeal was very largely to the specific in his age. Hence eighteenth and nineteenth century indifference, and hence the new appreciation of Donne's poetry which resulted from a certain similarity in the outlooks of the seventeenth and twentieth centuries.

But Donne's immediate influence was profound, and since it served to deepen the scope of the lyric, complementary to Jonson's, in spite of the seeming antagonism which drew from Jonson his "Donne for not keeping of accent deserves hanging." [41] Jonson's insistence on the classic and permanent virtues of restraint, simplicity, decorum, and good workmanship, was valuable as a corrective to the bad effect which such an individual style as Donne's might have had on his imitators. Both helped to bring a new sincerity into the lyric, Jonson by dispensing with the vain conceit, Donne by developing a new conceit, possessed of a new personal urgency and capable of expressing genuine, if highly intellectualized, emotion. Together they opposed Spenserian facility and Petrarchian affectation.

40 *Conversations with Drummond of Hawthornden*
41 *Conversations with Drummond of Hawthornden*

To follow out exhaustively the influence of Jonson's style on seventeenth century poetry would be unprofitable and, in fact, impossible. There is no extricating the two dominating influences of Donne and Jonson from their interplay throughout the period. The metre of Herrick's *Night Piece,* the movement of Carew's *Secrecy Protested,* the design of Suckling's *False One,* are obviously derived directly from Jonson's verse. But had his example produced nothing but surface imitation of this kind, it would have been of doubtful benefit. His influence is far more penetrating, more all-pervading, and is less concerned with superficialities than with the promotion in the work of his successors of the fundamental qualities which went to make his own supreme lyric success.

Compared to that of Donne or Milton, Jonson's originality was of a more impersonal type, less occupied in the creation of a purely or exclusively individual mode of utterance. The great individualists among the poets are a danger to their imitators: a Shakespearian or a Miltonic inflection may prove stifling to a lesser poet. But Jonson, through his absorption of the classical ideal, achieved an unusual negation of the accidentally personal. And his lyric style, in which alone he attains to perfect self-expression, exerts a force which, instead of overwhelming his followers in its personality, in its impersonality acts only on their art. It is this truth which becomes obscured if the Jonson of romantic biography, a forceful individual, arrogant, exclusive, sensitive to personal affront, is allowed to wield an undue influence on the critic of his art. And it is because this has been so in the past, to such a great extent, that so little genuine criticism has been brought to bear on it.

His influence on the eighteenth century was probably wider and more general, if less direct, than it had been on the seventeenth. He had prepared English poetry for the coming of the age of reason; he had done much towards enabling it to fulfil its new requirements; he had been the voice crying in the wilderness. And to the first genuine classical lyricist of

English poetry the debt of the English neo-classic lyric is naturally inestimable. But the eighteenth century never fully realized the significance of Ben Jonson's lyric success, never achieved his peculiar virtue of self-absorption in art, the perfect harmony between emotion and the process of creation which Jonson derived from his clearer conception of the underlying ideal of classical art.

Sometimes his poetry expresses a preconceived emotion; sometimes it embodies a conception of beauty which is typically Elizabethan; sometimes it employs the idiom of wit. But these are not intrinsic factors in his highest lyric success, and his poetry should not be valued merely, or chiefly, on their account. Prejudiced criticism detaches fragments illustrative of these qualities for special commendation, just as it concentrates on isolated passages of a similar kind in the plays, ignoring the essential artistic intention from which they are accidental divergences. It is of the utmost importance that Jonson's poetry should be judged as what it is, and by what it tries to be, not as something wholly different. His peculiar lyric achievement is a poetry which is, in its own way, "absolute." It cannot be considered as the product of an emotional mood detachable from itself; nor does it arouse one. The touchstone of "high seriousness" does not apply. The "subject," although it forms an integral part of the finished lyric, is not the predominant or determining factor in its composition. It is not what it says, but what it is, that matters. To this extent the philosophical meaning is irrelevant, let it be derived from Philostratus, from Catullus, or from chance. In its construction there is no opposition between art and inspiration, for art is its inspiration.

LITERARY CRITICISM IN JONSON'S CONVERSATIONS WITH DRUMMOND

Drummond's rough notes of Jonson's conversations with him at Hawthornden in 1618 are not only, as is always said, the chief source of information about the facts of Jonson's life and the best means we have for estimating the impact which his living personality made on his contemporaries, but they also contain statements about literature and life which make some addition to those in the *Discoveries* and Jonson's other works, and they must consequently be taken into account in any general survey of his thought. But unfortunately, in order to read these few scattered critical statements aright, some questions of character and circumstance do inevitably arise, however anxious we may be to avoid creating a fictional Ben Jonson to live in our minds half-independent of his works: for we are concerned here, not with the considered thoughts of a writer communicating with the world in general and posterity, but with casual talk spoken by one man who had no thought of its preservation, and reported by another who had no thought of its publication. The record has not passed through the filtering, adjusting process to which both speaker and writer would have subjected it if they had known that it would some day lie open to the scrutiny of the world as their joint production. It remains coloured by the idiosyncracies of the two personalities and by their not wholly sympathetic relationship; as appears most obviously, not in the reporting, but in the sweeping comment on it all contained in the famous paragraph where Drummond sums up his own impression of Ben Jonson.

Drummond's jottings do not read as if made from memory long afterwards, but as if he had, Boswell-like, made a nightly record of Jonson's talk while the very turn of his phrases remained fresh in mind. "Owen is a pure [poor] Pedantique Schoolmaster sweeping his living from the Posteriors of little children"; "My Lord Chancelor of England wringeth his speeches from the strings of his band & other Councellours from the pyking of thr teeth"; "Done for not keeping of accent deserved hanging"; such sentences have the accent of rapid and emphatic speech, caught and transferred to writing before its warmth could cool. I think it must be accepted that Drummond was as accurate and impartial as possible in his reporting of the actual words spoken, however much his prejudices may have influenced subconsciously the selection his memory made from them. But when he proceeds to evoke, in a few sentences at the end, his own sharply realized impression of the speaker, he is anything but impartial, and he may easily misdirect our attitude to the whole of what has gone before.

"He is a great lover and praiser of himself, a contemner and Scorner of others, given rather to losse a friend, than a Jest, jealous of every word and action of those about him (especiallie after drink, which is one of the Elements jn which he liveth) a dissembler of ill parts which raigne jn him, a bragger of some good that he wanteth, thinketh nothing well bot what either he himself, or some of his friends and Countrymen hath said or done. he is passionately kynde and angry, carelesse either to gaine or keep, Vindictive, but if he be well answered, at himself. for any religion as being versed in both: jnterpreteth best sayings and deeds often to the worst: oppressed with fantasie, which hath ever mastered his reason, a generall disease jn many poets."

There is no hint here of the humour, the playfulness, the exaggerating wit and deliberate rhetoric, which were surely the corrective elements in so much of what appears extravagant in Jonson's talk about himself and others. Coleridge, commenting on Jonson's recommendation to Drummond to read Hippocrates "for health," maintained that Drummond failed to see that this was merely intended as a joke: "But this is characteristic of a Scotchman; he has no notion of a jest unless you tell him 'This is a joke'." [1] How Coleridge could be certain that Drummond did not see it (if it *was* a joke) is not clear; but there are at least three statements in the paragraph just quoted which may be taken to indicate that Drummond was devoid of humour and so incapable of understanding Jonson. "Given rather to losse a friend, than a Jest" is a piece of self-criticism which Drummond naively repeats; it was satirically applied to Jonson by himself in the *Poetaster,* where Tucca says of Horace, "he will sooner lose his best friend, then his least iest".[2] It is impossible to accept literally "for any religion as being versed in both" as a description of a man with such integrity of mind where serious matters were concerned, and this must surely have been a playful comment by Jonson himself on the two changes he had made in the form of his religion, from Anglicanism to Catholicism and back. "Oppressed with fantasie which hath ever mastered his reason" may be an emphatic way of saying that his talk struck Drummond as more often fanciful than reasoned, but, since the word "ever" occurs in it, appears rather to be a confession by Jonson himself, and is probably no more than his own exaggerated comment on the highly coloured account he gives of his occasional sack-stimulated musings: "he heth consumed a whole night jn lying looking to his great toe, about which he hath seen tartars & turks Romans and Carthaginions feight in his jmagination."

Drummond, I suspect, was unable to appreciate the corrective and balancing critical undercurrent of Jonson's talk, which must have been conveyed by intonation, attitude, expression, and gesture; just as some of his later critics appear to have missed the critical undertones of his rhetorical and

1 *Notes on Ben Jonson,* 1818
2 *Poetaster,* IV, iii

imaginative writing. Perhaps he did not quite believe that Jonson would have condemned his friend Donne, "the first poet jn the World jn some things," to be hanged by the neck till he was dead, for taking licences with English prosody; yet he could dismiss as a "contemner and Scorner of others" the man who, in his hearing, gave generous though not undiscriminating approval to the works of Chapman, Donne, Spenser, Beaumont, Fletcher, Wotton, Hooker, Selden, and Southwell – to name only those mentioned who wrote in English – and who said of Drummond's own verses that they "were all good, especiallie my Epitaph of the Prince."

It is highly probable that Jonson, with his dramatist's sensitivity to character, was thoroughly conscious of Drummond's limitations: indeed he said so fairly plainly when he told him he "was too good and simple, and that oft a mans modestie, made a foot of his witt"; and that Drummond's innocence and reserve, touched in Jonson's eyes, perhaps, with a hint of prudery and priggishness, acted as an incitement to Jonson to dazzle and shock him with a display of sophistication. Much of what was said in rhetorical emphasis, and out of sheer high spirits, as well as a little of what we should nowadays call leg-pulling, was perhaps too solemnly accepted by Drummond as expressing the opinions and feelings of a man he felt bound to respect because of his eminence. For though Drummond belonged to the landed class, and was a man of birth, learning, and letters, as well as of substance, his guest, though poor and of uncertain ancestry, was a national celebrity, who had published two years before a handsome and bulky edition of his collected *Works* (which he assured Drummond did not contain "the half of his comedies") and who held a position at the head of the literary world which was all but official. Drummond was no doubt much in awe of him, and ill able to produce the suitable riposte to counter his more outrageous sallies or elicit tempering observations from him where his censure was too crudely expressed, as in the cases of Owen, Sharpham, Dekker, Minshieu, Fraunce, Markham, Day and

Middleton; yet Drummond had the penetration to observe that if "well answered" he was "at himself" to make amends for his overstatements. The unexpressed dissent, the pent-up disapproval, the humiliation of being patronized, lectured to, and overridden, may have found a natural relief in Drummond's secretly written condemnation of Jonson's character, with its single appreciative clause, so much more subtly revealing than all the rest.

Doing the best one can to discriminate between what was spoken in earnest and what Drummond was intended to take in jest; between what is exaggerated because of the immediate desire to impress a collocutor, and what seems to be the product of considered thought, one finds in the *Conversations* a number of statements which are well in keeping with the critical tenets expressed in the *Discoveries*. There is, of course, the pervasive concern to maintain standards in an age which Jonson sees as decadent, which sharpens his criticism everywhere, and which Drummond, accustomed no doubt to a courteous tolerance in critical discussions, or at any rate to more ceremonious forms of condemnation, seems to mistake for the censoriousness that springs from jealousy and conceit. Yet except where Jonson blurts out some expression of personal antipathy, dismissing Dekker as a rogue, Fraunce as a fool, or Markham as a base fellow, his adverse criticisms are usually specific, as where he objects to the stanza-form in the *Faerie Queene* and the intricacy of its allegory; to the want of "decorum" in Lucan, Sidney, and Guarini; to the unwieldy length of Drayton's lines in the *Polyolbion*; to the prosaic nature of Fairfax's alexandrines; to the failure of Harrington and Owen to grasp the distinction between an epigram and a narrative; and to the profane implications of Donne's *First Anniversary*. Where he refers to poetry in general he speaks as the habitual critic, concerned to maintain a scale of values in literary appreciation, in defiance of the world's indifference, and to assert not only the broader distinction between a poet and a "Balletmaker" but the finer one, which he learned from Aristotle and Quintilian, between a poet and a "Verser."

In the *Conversations* we may find some hint, too, of the preoccupation with sincerity in art as against superficial affectation, which is the counterpart to Jonson's moral preoccupation with personal integrity, or what he calls 'honesty,' in an age he considered peculiarly corrupted by hypocrisy. This, no doubt, is what dictates his comments on Spenser's style and language in the *Conversations* and in the *Discoveries,* and underlies the excellent criticism of Drummond's own verses "that they were all good . . . save that they smelled too much of the schooles and were not after the Fancie of the tyme," or, in other words, adopted the superficialities of the Petrarchan convention, which had long since outlived its early vitality. On the same score Jonson was naturally indignant to find passing as poetry such trivial ingenuities as acrostics, anagrams, and the fashionable shaped verses which were made to look like windows, crosses, hearts, and other objects:

> those finer flammes
> Of Egges, and Halberds, Cradles, and a Herse,
> A paire of Scisars, and a Combe in verse.[3]

He "scorned" them to Drummond, obviously, for the reason that they subjected the spirit to the form, the inspiration to the adopted convention, more rigorously even than the sonnet, the Procrustean bed which he cursed Petrarch for bringing into use – and making so fashionable, he might have added, that for a time it seems that almost every man who could use a pen was setting up to be a sonnetteer.

The doctrine that perspicuity is the principal virtue of style, preached in the *Discoveries* in opposition to a contemporary trend towards complexity and obscurity, is, of course, behind the comment "that Donne himself for not being understood would perish"; as also surely behind the objection to Spenser's allegory, which, as Jonson had observed, required exposition in the Letter to Sir Walter Raleigh instead of

3 *An Execration upon Vulcan* in *Underwoods*

carrying its full meaning in itself. And the doctrine of "body" in verse, or the paramountcy of sense, preached in the *Discoveries* in opposition to an older, but still surviving, predilection for trivial matter decked out in an affected style, is, I suspect, behind his high estimation of Donne (for all his obscurities and violations of the metrical niceties) as "the first poet jn the World jn some things." Between his insistence, reiterated in the *Discoveries,* on the value of simplicity in form and language, with attention to the graces of melody and shapeliness in so far as these are integral and not mere impositions, and his equal emphasis on the prime importance of the sense of what is said, there seems to have existed some incompatibility in his own mind, for he told Drummond "that Verses stood by sense without either Colour's or accent, which yett other tymes he denied." This conflict in Jonson's mind is a part of the growing-pain of literary criticism: he could not abandon either position, since both were necessary to his defence of sincerity in art, yet he had not at hand the philosophical resources, the linguistic instruments, with which to effect a reconciliation very easily made by the modern reader, who has been taught to recognize that meaning is a far more complex thing than sense.

In keeping, too, with the teaching of the *Discoveries* is the concern shown in the *Conversations* for "decorum," which, though applied always by Jonson in the narrower sense of the suitability of dialogue in fiction to the characters who speak it, might as well be used for the broader consideration of which that is a part — attention to fact, to probability, to the truths of nature, where their violation may disorganize or disrupt an imaginative conception. It is concern for "decorum" which leads him to complain that Sidney made his characters "speak as well as himself"; but it is also concern for decorum, in the broader sense, which leads him to object to Shakespeare's free and easy violation of geographical fact when he shipwrecks Antigonus and his company (as Greene had done before him) on the sea-coast of Bohemia. This casual comment, uttered in some context of talk which we do not know, seems to me neither so absurdly insensitive as Jonson's detractors have maintained, nor so pointlessly insignificant as his apologists suggest. It illustrates in a crudely obvious way the substance of what Jonson's criticism of Shakespeare, as expressed in the *Discoveries* as well as in the *Conversations,* appears to be — that the variability in his art was due to its insufficient control by the consciously critical activities of his mind. As Aristotle knew, the intrusion into the mind of a reader or hearer of a consideration for fact and probability, through their wanton or ignorant violation, may be disastrous, where the situation is a fanciful one and depends on the suspension for the time being of such considerations; it shows either want of art or want of common knowledge in the contriver, and if it produces an incongruous effect of absurdity, the full communication of his feelings and ideas must suffer interruption. Jonson had felt an incongruity of the sort in the ship-wreck scene in *The Winter's Tale* — so curiously botched, not only as to setting but in its whole shaping — and instanced it to Drummond, no doubt, as a case of "would he had blotted" like a more deliberate artist. His criticism of Shakespeare in the *Conversations* that he "wanted Arte" must not be understood to mean, surely, in view of what he says in the lines contributed to the First Folio edition, that he lacked art, but rather that his art was wanting in that conscious deliberation which might have rectified his occasional lapses.

Jonson's jesting comments on pictures reveal in the same way his preoccupation with "decorum" in the broad sense. Laughter is one way in which criticism may express itself, and "the greatest sport he saw jn France, was the picture of our saviour with the apostles eating the Pascall Lamb that was all Larded"— though how he could have been so certain of the lard is hard to see. Here, as in the remark about the "bed after the fashion of ours" in the picture of Esther, Haman, and Ahasuerus, the objection to a minor inaccuracy may seem a piece of over-scrupulous pedantry, though, without certainty as to what pictures he is referring to, we cannot tell to what extent these minor incongruities do disturb, for others, the harmony of their design. What we can say is that his hypersensitiveness to this particular sort of blemish is plainly related to his general conception of art as demanding the whole mind of the artist, in whom a mature intellect is in control of the impulses and whose imagination is enriched by knowledge and experience. It is the "civilized" conception of the artist and poet which he holds: the reverse of that extreme romantic view which sees them as creatures of impulse and inspiration, in whom the higher mental faculties are better to remain undeveloped, or at any rate unused.

There are signs, even in the *Conversations,* of the restlessly active and experimental nature of Jonson's genius. Like other original artists who, by their influence, have infused new vitality into the art they practised, he is a respecter of tradition but a breaker of convention. As a critic he tries to see through recent encrustations to the solid core of permanent worth in literature, and, as he indicates to Drummond, he studies Petronius, the younger Pliny, and Tacitus, because he finds something of permanent value in their styles; Quintilian and Horace, because they have something permanently valuable to say about the theory of art; Juvenal, Martial, Persius, and Pindar, because they stimulate thought and imagination. Yet he is no "neo-classic." The *Discoveries* show how far he is from believing that modern poetry must pattern itself on classical poetry or modern thought on classical thought, and his own attitude to his writing is well suggested by the various mottoes he used: *Tanquam Explorata* was the phrase inscribed on the books in his library, and he told Drummond that the word he had chosen to encircle his crest was "percunctabor [percunctator?] or perscrutator." His writing was that of an experimenter, an adventurer: in drama, poetry, and prose he is constantly engaged in exploring new modes conceived through his respect for tradition and his rejection of convention, in a conscious effort, by trial and error, to redirect the art of his time out of its shallowing channels into the deeper main stream, and by the example of his own energetic optimism for its future to infuse it with a new vitality. It strikes one as characteristic that so much of his talk to Drummond should have been of new literary projects of his own, in kinds of writing he had not, as far as we know, hitherto assayed: "he is to writt his foot pilgrimage hither & to call it a discoverie"; "he had ane jntention to perfect ane Epick Poeme jntitled Heroologia of the Worthies of his Country, rowsed by fame, and was to dedicate it to his Country"; "he heth intention to writt a fisher or Pastoral play & sett the stage of it jn the Lowmond Lake." Not all of these plans seem to have matured, yet his talk of them was not mere brag, as the subsequent correspondence with Drummond shows; and we know from the *Execration upon Vulcan* that the account of his journey to Scotland, written in verse, was among the papers destroyed in the burning of his library in 1623. It has never been explained why Jonson, at the age of forty-six, with his "hundred of Gray haires" and his "mountaine belly,"[4] should have set out to walk to Scotland and back, but the answer is probably implied in these very remarks: he went to Scotland (not without an eye, perhaps, to the advancement it might give him in King James's favour) to collect material and "local colour" for further experiments in new modes of writing.

The moralist of the *Discoveries* appears in the *Conversations,* as it were in undress, in such emphatic declarations as "He never esteemed of a man for the name of a Lord"; "he would not flatter though he saw Death";"of all stiles he loved most to be named honest." In the *Discoveries* it is chiefly on hypocrisy that he makes war, as moralist and as social critic — but also as literary critic; for to Jonson the connection between individual integrity, the health of society, and the voice of a healthy society expressed in the matter and manner of individual writers is so close that when discussing even the superficialities of literary technique his judgement can be seen to be

[4] *My Picture Left in Scotland,* in *Underwoods*

at bottom a moral one. This may be illustrated even from the scattered remarks on verse technique in the *Conversations,* for though we do not know precisely how he defended the couplet in the lost "discourse of Poesie both against Campion & Daniel especially this Last, wher he proves couplets to be the bravest sort of Verses," it is not difficult from his strictures on other forms of verse, to guess what line he took. The couplet commended itself to him as less prone to be employed for trivial and showy purposes than more intricate verse-forms. Even cross-rhyming and division into stanzas seemed to him dangerously apt to force the sense according to the pattern and so impose that false discipline from without which he connected with the sonnet and the Spenserian stanza and, at its absurd extreme, with those *Logogriphes, Palindromes, Anagrams, Eteostichs, Acrostichs,* and *Telestichs* held up to ridicule in the *Execration upon Vulcan.* It is easy to see from his own use of the couplet that he looked on it as a form which, while it possessed an ordered shapeliness, encouraged a peculiarly direct and unaffected kind of communication, and demanded that attention to "body" and "perspicuity" which he believed to constitute the necessary discipline from within that was so often lacking in an age whose hypocrisies were as clearly reflected in its literary styles as in the behaviour of individuals and the customs of society. That he "detesteth all other Rimes" but couplets is, of course, an overstatement to Drummond made in the course of a heated defence: his approving quotation of poems and passages in a variety of metres, his appreciative comments on verses not written in couplets, and his practice as a poet, which extended even to the effective use of the despised sonnet, are sufficient proof of that.

Behind the various instances I have given we may recognize in the speaker the writer of the *Discoveries;* but there are also, of course, asides which spring from the emotion of the moment, and were intended to die with it, and gestures suited to a temporary mood, which do not express the inmost essence of Jonson, like his complaints about his poverty, his boasts about his physical prowess, the display of his intimacies with his aristocratic patrons, and that jesting dissuasion from poetry, so ludicrously pointless considering Drummond's circumstances: "He dissuaded me from Poetrie, for that she had beggered him, when he might have been a rich lawyer, Physitian or Marchant." To trace in the *Conversations* the threads of the same thought that runs so clearly through the *Discoveries* we have to consider the nature of Drummond's conception of the man and the nature of Jonson's own reaction to it, and then to rid ourselves of any preoccupation with either — a process of detachment which might so often have been salutary in the past, not merely in discussing the *Conversations,* which have always been a special preserve of biographers and historians, but in the criticism of Jonson's other works, which his bulky, impressive, but enigmatic figure was for too long allowed to obscure.

Having passed through a phase of idolatry in the memory of his poetical progeny; a phase of reverential respect in the esteem of Augustan neo-classics; and a phase of something rather like contempt in the estimation of early romantic critics like Capell, Hurd, and Young, Jonson's works were of minor concern to later romantics, who occupied themselves, in preference, with his character. This suffered at first from detractors, pleased to find in Drummond's notes some moral justification for their general distaste for all they conceived him to stand for in literature; but after Gilchrist and Gifford had sprung to his defence he was sentimentalized anew. He was referred to affectionately by his Christian name, and thought of as a type, different from Marlowe, Sidney, or Raleigh, but just as representative of the romantic Elizabethan; vivacious, pushing, jolly, temperamental, and given to flouting the conventions of morality and respectability in a commendably "escapist" way. His personality mattered more than his works, for, unlike Shakespeare, he had obligingly stamped its outlines on the imagination of his time so that they endured, and could be filled in with high colours; but even his works acquired, in the light of this romantic conception of the man, a new limited interest; for they were found to possess romantic qualities, his blank verse to be not far inferior to Marlowe's when it reached rhetorical heights, his lyrics to show an occasional glimmer of that enchantment it was sacrilege to analyse, his *Sad Shepherd* to contain Arcadian fancies that justified the belief that he might have written comedies more gracefully "poetical" than his humour plays if he had struck the vein in time. The friendly admiration for a rollicking good fellow, formidable in learned controversy but essentially good-hearted, all the more likeable because his faults are so apparent, which colours the attitude of the nineteenth century towards Jonson's writing, persisted until recently, and is not absent from such finely critical biographies as those of A. H. Thorndike, Gregory Smith, and John Palmer, though rigorously expunged from the essays on Jonson by Mr. T. S. Eliot and Mr. L. C. Knights.

No doubt, in the multiplicity of his nature he was many men in one – as we all are; though not being all of us actors and dramatists, we may be content to play one part or few where he amused himself by playing many. Biographers and novelists may make almost anything they please of him, provided the figure is learned, energetic, and indomitable: it may be in the main attractive, or in the main repulsive, and in both cases appear to fit the ascertainable facts. But it is well to remember that we can never know the man, though we may fancy we understand him better than Drummond did; and that what must matter most to us is not his personality, however fascinating in its elusiveness, but the poetry and prose in which he sought to express his conception of the permanently true and beautiful – nothing so imperfect and ephemeral as a personality.

DATE DUE

APR 5 1986			
APR 8 REC'D			
MAY 6 1986			
MAY 1 REC'D			